Acts of an Awesome God:

OUT OF DARKNESS

McDougal & Associates

Servants of Christ and Stewards of the
Mysteries of God

Acts of an Awesome God:

OUT OF DARKNESS

by

Jim O. Richardson

Published by:

McDougal & Associates
18896 Greenwell Springs Road
Greenwell Springs, LA 70739

www.thepublishedword.com

McDougal & Associates is an organization dedicated to spreading the Gospel of the Lord Jesus Christ to as many people as possible in the shortest time possible.

ISBN: 978-1-940461-81-6

Printed in the U.S., the U.K. and Australia
For Worldwide Distribution

But you are a chosen generation, a royal priesthood, a holy nation, His own special people, that you may proclaim the praises of Him who called you **OUT OF DARKNESS** *into His marvelous light.*
1 Peter 2:9

Dedication

This book is dedicated to all sincere seekers of the truth. Truth is what it is; it is not merely what you want it to be. In order to know the truth, we must be willing to set aside our preconceived notions and allow our hearts and minds to embrace new things we discover along the way.

As you read the stories in this book, you may have your theology challenged, but you will also have your faith stirred and your hope restored. In these pages you will read about true accounts of God's incredible love, mercy, forgiveness and restoration. You will also come to know a God of amazing power who still moves in absolutely incredible ways on behalf of those who seek Him out of a sincere and humble heart.

Be blessed, be encouraged and be strengthened by these astounding *Acts of an Awesome God*!

Contents

INTRODUCTION

In the Bible, God is referred to as *"the Father of Lights"* [1] and with good reason. Since the beginning of time He has been about the business of dispelling darkness by introducing various types of illumination into the world.

In the very first chapter of Genesis, the Bible tells us:

> *The earth was without form, and void; and darkness was on the face of the deep. And the Spirit of God was hovering over the face of the waters. Then God said, "Let there be light"; and there was light ... . and God divided the light from the darkness.*   Genesis 1:2-4

Multiple centuries passed, and God's Spirit once again hovered over the earth. But this time, instead of creating a natural source of light to drive dark-

---

1. James 1:17

ness from the surface of the planet, God would create a spiritual source of light that would drive darkness from the hearts of humanity. The name of this magnificent light? Jesus Christ, the Son of God.

Referring to Christ's illuminating effect on humanity, John declared:

> *In Him was life, and the life was the light of men. And the light shines in the darkness ..... That was the true Light which gives light to every man coming into the world.*
>
> John 1:4-5 and 9

We find a similar description of Jesus in Matthew:

> *The people who sat in darkness have seen a great light,*
> *And upon those who sat in the region and shadow of death Light has dawned.*
>
> Matthew 4:16

Jesus came to earth in order to restore mankind to the light and life which can only be found through fellowship with God, a fellowship that had been broken through Adam and Eve's disobedience in the Garden of Eden.

INTRODUCTION

During His time on earth, Jesus was constantly calling people out of spiritual darkness, and today, by the power of the Holy Spirit, people are still being called out of darkness and introduced to the light and life found only through God's Son.

I know because it happened to me. This is my story.

Jim O. Richardson

Chapter 1

DRAWN OUT OF DARKNESS

Jesus therefore answered and said to them, "...
No one can come to Me unless the Father who
sent me draws him."   John 6:43-44

I've heard countless Christians say over the years that one day they just "decided" to come to the Lord. According to John 6:44, that just isn't true. The fact is, we aren't capable of making a decision to become a Christian on our own, and, apart from God's drawing and the Holy Spirit's enlightenment, we never will be. The act of becoming a Christian is a spiritual experience and, by its very nature, is beyond the ability of mere human intellect or mental reasoning to fully comprehend.

The Bible says it this way in First Corinthians:

But the natural man does not receive the things
of the Spirit of God, for they are foolishness to

him; nor can he know them, because they are spiritually discerned.   1 Corinthians 2:14

Knowing we will never voluntarily give up the lures and attractions of this world to pursue Him, due to our limited capacity to comprehend the wonderful gifts He has in store for those who serve Him, God the Father takes the initiative to draw each one of us out of spiritual darkness and into a personal relationship with Himself. In my own case, God began the process of drawing me to Him early in life.

Exposure to the Light

I was raised during the 1950s in a small rural community in South Central Oklahoma. Back in those days my hometown was a popular stopping place for sawdust evangelists who would pitch their large tents in vacant lots or empty fields around town. Occasionally curiosity would get the best of me, and I would stop by one of those huge tents while a service was in full swing. Sometimes I even mustered up enough courage to peek inside, but most of the time I just stood outside the open flaps which served as a front door to those canvas tabernacles.

DRAWN OUT OF DARKNESS

I would listen intently while the ministers preached fiery sermons, ranging from the wages of sin and eternal damnation, to the love of God and the plan of salvation. As interested as I was, and as compelling as some of the evangelistic messages sounded, I never responded by making the decision to become a Christian myself. God was calling, but I wasn't answering.

Then, when I was about ten, a close friend invited me to visit the small Baptist church he attended. I liked the people there and began to go to Sunday School regularly, where I learned about God and the Bible in a much deeper way. I even learned the books of the Bible, which I could proudly recite in chronological order.

One Sunday after Sunday School class had ended, instead of staying for the morning service, I decided to go home early. While crossing a long bridge over a deep creek on the way to our house, I was struck by a car. The impact resulted in some major scrapes and cuts (requiring several stitches) and a few broken bones, which caused me to be laid up at home for the next several weeks. For some reason, after I recovered from that accident, I didn't return to the Baptist church.

Over the next few years I attended one service at a Church of the Nazarene (at the request of a close friend), a midnight mass at a Catholic church (in response to an invitation from a girlfriend), and, for a short time, I accompanied a classmate and his family while they attended services at a local Assembly of God church. Yet, for all the messages I heard taught at Sunday School and all the sermons I heard preached from pulpits over those early years, I never felt the desire to completely yield my life to God. All that changed when I reached the age of fifteen. That was when I met Kenny.

Kenny was a very popular guy at school, and, as I was soon to find out, a devoted Christian as well. He and I became friends, and one day he invited me to attend a youth service at the local First United Methodist Church. I decided to take Kenny up on his offer, and, at the end of one of the services, during the altar call, I felt compelled to go down to the front of the church for prayer.

After the service, I met with the pastor and stated my desire to live for God. I left the church that night feeling good about myself and determined to make a positive change in my life.

Slipping into Darkness

Unfortunately, since I did not maintain much-needed fellowship with other Christians, and had no one at home to encourage me in my walk with God, this new-found commitment didn't last very long. Jesus said, *"The spirit indeed is willing, but the flesh is weak"* (Matthew 26:41), and, sure enough, my will power alone proved insufficient to keep me walking on the straight and narrow path. Little by little, I turned back to sinful ways and grew increasingly worse with time.

In high school I began to hang out with the wrong crowd and occasional alcohol use progressed to frequent consumption, and it wasn't long before I began to experiment with drugs as well. One by one I began to engage in a number of illegal activities and was arrested several times. I never received any jail time for these crimes I committed, but one day things finally caught up with me, and I found myself behind bars once again, only this time I was facing felony charges for possession of a stolen vehicle.

I went to trial and, instead of being released as in times past with little more than a slap on the wrist, I was sentenced to spend an eight-month stretch in the county jail.

After several weeks of being locked up, I began to look back over the last few years of my life. I had been doing things that I knew were wrong, but it had seemed like I just couldn't stop. It was as if I was being controlled by an unseen force to commit these crimes against my better judgment.

Feeling powerless to make a change in my life, I finally cried out to God for help. Not long after that I felt an urge to begin studying the Bible.

Off and on, over the next several weeks, ministers from different denominations would visit the jailhouse on Sunday mornings and stand outside the cell bars preaching and teaching. As much as I appreciated their visits, it seemed that their message always fell a little short. One day I asked one of them if God still did miracles and healed people, as Jesus had done in the Bible. The minister informed me that those days had passed. "Today we are to simply live by faith," he explained.

"Then I don't need your God," I replied sharply. "Sounds to me like He can't do any more than a normal man!"

But what might have sounded like a disrespectful attitude toward God was actually my frustration toward man. Here I was, hungry to know more about the God of the Bible and experience the power of His presence, and these well-meaning ministers were offering me little more than I already knew.

A Vision in the Night

I continued my personal search for a deeper knowledge of God, and one night I had a very unusual dream. I saw myself standing on a rocky, barren hill. The sky was gray and overcast. Some distance away from me I saw another barren hill strewn with what appeared to be the ruins of Roman buildings. At the top of that hill was a man sitting on a white horse. He had a dark beard and long hair, wore a white robe and had a sword in his right hand. As I gazed at him, he suddenly reared the horse straight up, thrust his sword high into the air and yelled out, "Excelsior!" The sound of that word echoed across the deep chasm that separated us and rang in my ears.

When I awoke, I knew that dream had a special meaning. I looked up the word *excelsior* in the dictionary, and, to my surprise, found it was of Latin origin and meant "reach higher." (It is significant to note here that Latin was the language of the Romans who controlled the Holy Land during Jesus' day, which would explain the Latin word He spoke to me and the Roman ruins I saw in my dream. It is also interesting to note that the words Pilate wrote and had placed over Jesus on the cross, "JESUS OF

NAZARETH, THE KING OF THE JEWS," were written in Latin, as well as Greek and Hebrew. Also significant in that dream was the fact that Jesus sat on a majestic white horse (the steed of a conqueror), high atop a hill, while the marble columns of an ancient civilization lay scattered below (significant of the fall of the mighty Roman Empire.) I was confident this message was from God and that He was telling me to keep reaching higher in my search to know Him better.

The only God I had come to know over the years was what I refer to as a "watered-down" version. He was still holy and divine all right, yet, from what I had been taught, He had ceased to move anymore in the supernatural and miraculous.

But what kind of a God is that? I thought. After all, moving in the supernatural was what made Him God. So why and when did He stop performing miracles? Something deep within me just couldn't accept the concept of a powerless God. Finally, one day I reached the point where I simply had to know the truth.

My Damascus Road Experience

I had just finished eating lunch one day and sat down on my jail bunk for my daily scripture reading.

DRAWN OUT OF DARKNESS

After a few minutes of study, I slid the Bible aside and stood up. Looking between the gray, steel bars of my cell, I peered out the window.

The jail was located on the top floor of an old four-story courthouse, so I was provided with a relatively unobstructed view to the north. It was just past noon, and although it was a cold winter's day, the sky was clear, except for two small white clouds that floated lazily along in the bright blue sky. As I fixed my gaze on those small clouds, I spoke from my heart these simple, yet sincere words: "God, I believe You're real. I don't have any problem with that. But what I want to know is if You still move in awesome, supernatural power like You did in the days of the apostles.

"Now, if I'm being like the heathen who seek after a sign," [2] I continued, "then I ask You to forgive me because I'm ignorant and don't know any better." I ended my prayer with the words, "Thank You, God. Amen!"

After I prayed this prayer, I just stood there for a while watching those two tiny clouds slowly drifting along. It couldn't have been more than thirty seconds after I finished that brief prayer that a very large, bright light suddenly appeared at the lower right side of my peripheral vision. It lasted only a moment, and it was gone.

2. See Matthew 12:38-39

I glanced down in the direction from where I thought the light had shone. It seemed to have come from directly in front of a tall stained-glass cross which was slightly recessed in the south wall of a large Methodist church located just a block from the Court House. It was the very same church where I had an encounter with God during that youth service seven years before.

I have observed something very special about God. After we have drifted away from Him, He will often take us back to a time and place where we once had an experience with Him, in order to reestablish a relationship with us. This is His loving way of getting us back on the right path.

We have a prime example of this in the New Testament. It was on the shore of the Sea of Galilee that Jesus stood when He first called Peter to follow Him, and Peter followed Him faithfully for many months. Then, just before Christ's crucifixion, Peter denied even knowing the Lord. After His resurrection, Jesus appeared to Peter again on the shore and beckoned to him again, *"Follow me"* (John 21:19).

Paul wrote to the Romans, *"Who shall separate us from the love of Christ?"* (Romans 8:35). So, if you have made a mistake, maybe many mistakes (as I have), I'm encouraging you not to give up on yourself or God. He's not through with you yet.

Believing that I might have just witnessed a supernatural event and not wanting to let this opportunity pass me by, I spoke to God again. This time I said, "God, I *thought* I just saw that cross light up. Could You do that for me one more time?" Only a matter of seconds passed before a blazing white light appeared. This time I was staring directly at the cross. The light was so massive that it blotted out the entire south wall of the church (which was half a city block wide), and it was the brightest, purest light I had ever seen in my life.

I didn't know anything could be that white. The light was so pure and white that, once its rays were gone, the midday sun appeared a dingy yellow in comparison.

You might think I should have been shocked by what I had seen, but, for some reason, I wasn't. Instead, I remarked to God very matter-of-factly, "That's good enough." Then I went on about my regular daily jail routine, as calm as I could be.

Many skeptics don't believe that you can call on God and realistically expect Him to answer in any meaningful way, but the Scriptures don't support that opinion. In fact, the prophet Jeremiah shows us that God Himself encourages us to do that very thing. He said:

> *Call to Me, and I will answer you, and show you great and mighty things which you DO NOT KNOW* [or, have never experienced].
> Jeremiah 33:3, Emphasis Added

I chose to keep this supernatural encounter to myself and continued to study the Bible over the following weeks. But that experience settled in my heart and mind, once and for all, two things:

1. That God is real, and
2. That He has not changed.

The Bible bears out God's unchanging nature. Referring to Himself, God said:

> *For I Am the LORD, I do not change.*
> Malachi 3:6

Something I have learned over the years is that if a spiritual experience is truly from God, He will confirm it to you in more ways than one. In a court of law, it takes two witnesses to establish a truth, and God uses a similar approach. The Bible says it this way:

> *By the mouth of two or three witnesses every word shall be established.*
>
> 2 Corinthians 13:1

God will use two or more methods to confirm whether the experience you have had is truly from Him or not, for He wants you to be confident and secure in your decisions and beliefs. He uses confirmations to help you know what and whom to trust.

One day God provided me with a confirmation of my encounter with that bright light as I was reading in the New Testament. In the 26th chapter of Acts, I came across a set of scriptures which recounted a similar experience a man had some two thousand years before. The Apostle Paul, while speaking to King Agrippa, began to recall an encounter he experienced while traveling on the road to Damascus:

> *at midday, O king, along the road I saw a light from heaven, BRIGHTER THAN THE SUN.*   Acts 26:13, Emphasis Added

Midday was exactly when this incredible vision had appeared to me too, and the light I saw was also brighter than the sun.

As I continued studying in the New Testament, I found yet another interesting confirmation to one aspect of my vision. As I said before, the light I saw was whiter than anything I had ever encountered. A similar supernatural brilliance is described by Mark in his gospel:

> *Now after six days Jesus took Peter, James and John, and led them up on a high mountain apart by themselves; and He was transfigured before them. His clothes became SHINING, EXCEEDINGLY WHITE, like snow, such as NO LAUNDERER ON EARTH can whiten them.* Mark 9:2-3, Emphasis Added

You may wonder why this spectacular event happened to me in particular. To be honest with you, I have often wondered about that myself. Maybe it was because I was a person to whom it was hard to prove something, and I usually tended to lean more toward a skeptical view of the claims of others. Maybe it was because I had been exposed to so many different theological doctrines and views throughout my life, and God had to set the record straight Himself. Or maybe it was because He wanted people to know the truth, and He knew I would someday be just the kind of person who would be willing to write a book about it.

One thing is for sure: God's choice wasn't based on my noble heritage. My family had no claim to fame or fortune and, in most cases, it was quite the contrary. Obviously, it wasn't because I was of such high personal moral character that God visited me. After all, I *was* in jail for a felony when this miracle occurred.

We must realize, however, that God doesn't see things the way we do, and He also doesn't select candidates the way we would. Despite all my shortcomings, I met very well God's scriptural selection requirements outlined by Paul in his first letter to the Corinthians:

> *For you see your calling, brethren, that not many wise according to the flesh, not many mighty, not many noble, are called. But God has chosen the foolish things of the world to put to shame the wise, and God has chosen the weak things of the world to put to shame the things which are mighty; and the base things*

of the world and the things which are despised
God has chosen, and the things which are not,
to bring to nothing the things that are, that no
flesh should glory in His presence.

1 Corinthians 1:26-29

Over the next few months I kept my mind focused on the things of God and was even used to provide words of comfort and encouragement to visitors and fellow prisoners. I continued to study the Bible, desiring to learn more about God.

After I completed my jail sentence, I was released and instantly set about to get my life moving in the right direction. I began to attend church, and, for a while at least, everything seemed to be going well. But we have an enemy of our soul who wastes no time and will spare no effort to get us away from the things of God. In the Parable of the Sower, Jesus explained it this way:

The seed is the word of God. Those by the
wayside are the ones who hear; then the devil
comes and takes away the word out of their
hearts, lest they should believe and be saved.

Luke 8:11-12

The seed of God's Word had already been planted in my soul there, but the devil was doing his best to make sure I would not totally yield my life to God. I soon quit attending services and did not seek any fellowship with other believers outside the church walls.

Over the next few years, I held down various jobs in Oklahoma and then spent several months working in Kansas. At first, things seemed to be going very well for me in Kansas, but the devil got a foothold in my life there too (wicked people and sinful opportunities are everywhere), and situations quickly went from bad to worse. It seemed the only thing to do was to move back home, so I ended up in Oklahoma once again.

Unfortunately, I hooked back up with many of my old acquaintances, none of whom encouraged me to seek after godly things. My life steadily declined into a regular weekly schedule of drugs, booze, parties and clubs until it seemed as if I was at the point of no return. The glorious vision I had encountered in jail years earlier almost appeared to be a wasted effort on God's part.

Then, two months before my 28th birthday, the Great Shepherd, true to His Word, left *"the ninety-nine"* (Luke 15:4), so that He could bring this one lost sheep back home. Fittingly, it happened early one Sunday morning.

My Day of Visitation

On this most unforgettable day, I was at the home of my older brother, Gary, who lived on the north side of Oklahoma City. I had just awakened in his den, after a night of intense partying. In an effort to help me clear my head, I decided to roll up a marijuana joint. I was in the process of trying to twist together the ends of the rolling paper when I began coughing so hard it shook the marijuana out of the paper and down onto a tray in my lap containing the rest of the pot and other drug paraphernalia.

Well, I don't guess I need any pot this morning, I said to myself, concluding the obvious. (After all, consuming large amounts of marijuana smoke over the last forty-eight hours was the reason I was coughing so hard in the first place). *Maybe I need a drink of liquor instead.*

With that, I got up and started into the kitchen where I set a bottle of whiskey on the table and prepared to pour myself a drink. As I stood over the bottle, I unscrewed the cap, and the pungent odor of alcohol that drifted up to my nostrils made me instantly nauseated. *Well, maybe I don't need anything to drink either,* I reasoned. *Maybe I just need to fix myself something to eat.*

Before I set about to prepare a meal, I decided to walk into the living room and see what was on the television. Much to my delight, a Christian music program was on. It was called "The Gospel Singing Jubilee," and it featured Southern Gospel vocal groups that I had greatly enjoyed listening to when I was younger. (I may have been deeply involved in a sinful lifestyle at the time, but I still could appreciate the uplifting nature of traditional Christian music).

As I headed back into the kitchen to prepare some breakfast, I stumped my toe on the coffee table in the middle of the living room floor. The experience was quite painful (if it has ever happened to you, then you know what I mean), and I let out a long string of choice curse words. It was at this point that everything began to get very strange.

A Holy Encounter

No sooner had I blurted out those foul words than an inner voice said to me, "There is a priest standing behind you, and he just heard every word you said. Now, what do you think about that?" This seemed like an especially unusual thought to me since most of my religious experiences involved ministers who did not carry the title of "priest."

To make the experience even stranger, I now had the overwhelming sensation of a holy presence and felt that this "priest" was actually standing in the living room looking at me at that very moment. (You might have had that eerie feeling before, too, like you're being watched.)

If everything wasn't odd enough already, I suddenly had a clear mental image of a man with dark shoulder-length hair and dark beard, dressed in a three-layered, multi-colored garment of a style I had never seen before. It wasn't until years later, during a time of Bible study that I discovered that the garments the Jewish High Priest wore during Old Testament times were actually similar to this mental image I had seen.

The picture in my mind was so vivid, and the presence in the room was so strong that I fully expected to turn and see this "holy man" actually standing behind me. Although I was apprehensive at what I might see, I nevertheless felt strongly compelled to look. I slowly turned around, only to find myself completely alone in the room. I wish I would have known at the time what the Scriptures say about Jesus in Hebrews:

DRAWN OUT OF DARKNESS

But He, because He continues forever, has an unchangeable priesthood. Therefore He is able to save to the uttermost those who come to God through Him, since He always lives to make intercession for them. Hebrews 7:24-25

If I had known that passage, I would have realized that Jesus Himself was standing in the room with me at that very moment, dealing with me about the sinful condition of my heart. While I realized that what had just happened was very strange, I tried to brush off the experience and continued into the kitchen.

I had only taken a few more steps when a second unsettling phrase clearly came to me. "Would you like for your nieces (who at the time were very young and asleep in their bedroom down the hallway) to hear you say those curse words?" the inner voice asked. I loved my nieces very much, and cursing is one of the things I made sure never to do around them, so this thought was especially troubling to me.

By this time, I was getting really perplexed at what was happening and said to myself, "What the heck is going on?" Since I really couldn't explain what had taken place in the living room, I attempted to forget about it for the time being and immediately set about to fix myself something to eat.

Everyone else who had been asleep in the house eventually began to stir, and the rest of the day progressed in a fairly uneventful manner. I thought I had put the whole experience behind me, but what I didn't know at the time was that God was far from finished with me. In fact, He quickly began to (what I have often looked back on and referred to as) "set me up" for a life-changing encounter with Him.

A Spiritual House Cleaning

Very soon I would become a full-fledged, born-again Christian. But before God would allow me to share in personal fellowship with Him, He would first clean the house, which His most Holy Spirit was about to inhabit. To accomplish this, God took me through a process over the next seven days, of which I was totally unaware at the time. It was such a smooth and comfortable transition that I didn't even know it was taking place.

It all started when I began to stop practicing some of my ungodly ways (though I thought at the time this was only to be temporary). And, all along, I thought *I* was the one making the decisions. But God, in His love and by His wisdom, was helping me do something I couldn't (and at the time didn't want to) do by myself. Day by day, things began to improve in my life.

I decided to stop drinking for a few days (I certainly had no plans of quitting for good. After all, why should I? My carnal nature was thoroughly enjoying all the sins I was indulging in at the time). I figured it would make me feel better if I cut back for a while, and, besides, it would help get my body back in shape so I could party even harder the next weekend.

I began feeling so good after abstaining from alcohol for that short time that I thought to myself, *I don't think I'll smoke any pot for a while either. That should really get me charged up for the weekend.*

If you've not come to this realization by now in your own life, you need to know that when the devil sees you trying to make the right decisions and do things God's way (even when you're not fully aware that it's actually Him giving you the motivation), that deceiver will quickly set out to ruin your plans. Be aware, too, that Satan has a wide variety of methods he uses and will oftentimes work through those closest to you to accomplish his sinister desires.

For example, when I decided not to smoke any pot for a while, I suddenly had unique opportunities come along for me to partake of, not only high-quality marijuana, but absolutely *free* marijuana.

Without my knowledge of it, my brother Gary had been cultivating a patch of marijuana on the outskirts of town and (coincidently) decided to harvest the hemp plants that very week. Naturally, he asked me to sample some of it with him. Uncharacteristically for me, I politely passed on the offer, saying that I would smoke some of it later. At least, that's what I thought.

The next day an old friend of mine showed up unexpectedly and offered me a free ounce of Panama Red. For those who are uniformed or inexperienced with the drug culture, Panama Red was one of the most potent types of marijuana ever to circulate in the U.S. drug market. When this offer came my way, a little light suddenly went off inside of me. *This is just a little TOO strange,* I thought. After all, standing in front of me was one of the stingiest people I had ever known, and he was suddenly offering me a very expensive bag of marijuana *absolutely free*! (You would have to have known this guy as well as I did to understand my utter shock at his unusually generous offer). I was *really* starting to question what was happening. As I had done with my brother earlier, I turned down my friend's offer for the free marijuana, much to his surprise (and mine too).

Along with curbing my drinking and smoking, sometime during the week I also came to another conclusion: "I think I'll try to cut down on my cursing," I said to my brother.

"That sounds like a good idea," he replied matter-of-factly.

Since God knew I was soon to make a confession of faith, I believe that He had begun the process of cleaning up my mouth in preparation for that holy moment. Again, all of this was happening without my understanding, and it clearly wasn't me who was making all these decisions; it was God working through me.

The Scriptures bear this out:

> *for it is God who works in you both to will and to do for His good pleasure.*
>
> Philippians 2:13

Chances are, if God would have told me what was going on, I might very well have rebelled in my typical carnal fashion and blown the chance of a lifetime. That's just human nature.

That week seemed to pass very quickly, and the weekend rolled around before I knew it. I decided I would head back south to my hometown to see my

friends and stay at the home of my maternal grandmother, who had raised me. Everyone affectionately
called her Granny.

Chapter 2

COMING BACK TO THE LIGHT

Train up a child in the way he should go,
And when he is old he will not depart from it.
                                            Proverbs 22:6

I spent Saturday night at Granny's, and by the time I woke up the next morning it was already past 11:00. As I lay in bed, I heard the voice of my long-time friend, Merrell, at the door. He lived only one block away and had come over to see what I had planned for the day.

Merrell entered the bedroom and asked me what I was going to do, and I said to him, "Actually, I was just thinking about going to church."

"Where at?" he asked.

"I was thinking about going to our old Baptist church," I replied.

"I'll go with you if you want to go," Merrell said.

That little Baptist Church was very special to both Merrell and me, although neither one of us had darkened its doors in a long while. Merrell had attended there for years while growing up, and his father, Gene, had helped found the church, led the song service, drove the church bus and served as a Sunday School teacher.

It was actually Gene who had taught me the books of the Bible in a small classroom in the southeast corner of that very church about seventeen years earlier. That was the last time I had attended services there.

Then, over the years, Gene had watched me grow up and saw my life steadily taking a downhill slide. I'm sure that, from his perspective, things didn't look very promising for me. A good thing to remember is to never become discouraged if you share the Word of God with someone and don't see immediate results. Your responsibility as a Christian is just to do whatever God lays on your heart, whether it is teaching Sunday School, sharing a personal testimony or simply doing a kind deed. God will always have another of His servants come along later—someday, somewhere—to add to that word. Then, at just the right time, God will do what only He can do—bring forth the fruits of righteousness.

The apostle Paul said it this way in his first letter to the Corinthians:

Who then is Paul, and who is Apollos, but ministers through whom you believed, as the Lord gave to each one? I planted, Apollos watered, but God gave the increase.

1 Corinthians 3:5-6

The seeds of salvation had been planted and watered in my life throughout the years by various preachers and believers, and all that was left now was for me to make my way to church so that God could complete the process.

Several times over the years different ministers had asked me if I wanted to give my heart to the Lord, and I would often respond, "I'm not ready yet, but when it's my time, I'll know." I was soon to find out that *this* was my time!

To everything there is a season,
A time for every purpose under Heaven.

Ecclesiastes 3:1

Outward Appearances

Having the traditional upbringing that I did, I was taught you should always look your best for church. The only problem was that I didn't have any dress clothes at Granny's house. The closest thing I could find that morning was an old pair of scuffed brown lace-up shoes that had belonged to my late grandfather (they were about a size and a half too big for me), one of his old white shirts (which was badly wrinkled) and a pair of old blue jeans. Although I was certain I wouldn't be dressed as nice as the other people I would see at church later that morning, I knew I was doing the best I could with what I had.

Over the years I have discovered that God is not nearly as interested in the condition of our wardrobe as people seem to be. God is more concerned with the condition of our heart. The Bible confirms this in First Samuel:

> *For the LORD does not see as man sees; for man looks at the outward appearance, but the LORD looks at the heart.* 1 Samuel 16:7

The devil has often used the thought of "not having anything to wear" to keep people out of church and, unknowingly, they have missed out on multiple blessings from God by giving in to this old trick of the enemy. But I was not about to be robbed of the greatest joy I would ever experience in life. I had made up my mind to attend Sunday morning service and so, dressed as I was, I headed off to church with absolutely no idea of what lay in store for me.

Becoming a New Creation

When Merrell and I arrived at the church, the service was almost over, but God is never late, and the timing couldn't have been better. I was able to hear the last part of the pastor's message and, to be honest with you, I can't even tell you what it was about. What I can tell you is that I suddenly began to feel a heat come all over me, and I became acutely aware of my sinful condition and that I needed a change in my life right then and there. Hot tears were streaming down my face and dripping onto the old Teacher's Bible lying in my lap. Granny had given it to me years before, in the hopes that I would one day draw strength and wisdom from its blessed pages.

The pastor gave the altar call and asked the most important question any human could ever hear spoken: "Would you like to come down to the front and invite Jesus into your heart?" Like so many other people who have found themselves in the same situation, I wanted to go to the front but just couldn't get myself to move. I can't tell you how important it is to have friends who will encourage you to do the right thing when you're having trouble making a vital decision like this on your own. I never said a word to Merrell, but somehow he seemed to know exactly what was going on inside of me. He leaned over and asked quietly, "Do you want to go to the front?"

"Yes," I said, sobbing, my lips quivering.

"Come on, I'll go with you," he assured me.

We got up from the pew and headed down to the front of the church, and there, with Merrell standing beside me, the pastor led me and the few others who had responded to his plea in the sinner's prayer. It was at that moment that I, as sincere as I had ever been in all my life, publicly accepted Jesus Christ as the Lord of my life and Savior of my soul. That decision was destined to change my life forever.

Before the service ended, the pastor announced that they would be holding a water baptism at six p.m. that evening for those who had accepted Christ that morning. I wanted to comply with everything I thought the Bible required of me, so I waited anxiously for the evening service. I was so excited about the prospect of being baptized in water that I went around that afternoon asking those nearest and dearest to me to be sure and be there to share with me in this very wonderful and special occasion.

COMING BACK TO THE LIGHT

When I got to church that night, I was in for a surprise. Of all the people who had gone forward that morning to accept Christ, I was the only one who had returned to take part in the water baptismal service. The Word of salvation had been planted in the hearts of five people that morning, but Satan had wasted no time in hindering the work of God's Spirit before it could take its full course in the lives of the other four.

The Parable of the Sower brings this fact to light. In this story, Jesus compares Himself to a farmer and the Word of God to His seed:

> *These likewise are the ones* [seeds] *sown on stony ground who, when they hear the Word, immediately receive it with gladness; and they have no root in themselves, and so endure only for a time.*   Mark 4:16-17

Satan's desire is to keep us away from God entirely, but if he can't do that, he will intervene at any point along the way in our lives that he can to stop us short of walking in total obedience to God's Word. This, he knows all too well, can cause us to miss out on God's fullest blessings.

The people who had come to the front with me that Sunday morning probably had good intentions and apparently saw a need for a change in their life, but other "things" had caused them to stop short of participating in the baptismal service. I acknowledge that there is no magic in baptismal water itself. The ceremony, nevertheless, serves as a powerful public statement of our commitment to serve God and can help strengthen our faith to live for Him.

To this day I am convinced that those four should have been at the baptism service that night because, over the next several months and throughout the following years, I watched as each of their lives steadily began to unravel, resulting in them falling back into their old defeated lifestyles.

A Fresh Start

From the moment I accepted Christ into my heart, things began to quickly change in my life. Among other things, the desire to habitually drink alcohol, take drugs, curse and live a wild lifestyle instantly left. And I do mean instantly!

It was truly a miraculous conversion. The Bible shows us that we can know people *"by their fruits,"* [3] and everyone who had known me for any amount of time knew that an incredible change had taken place

---

3. Matthew 7:16

in my life. This was evident by the positive fruit my life now produced. In fact, my very countenance was so totally altered that old friends and family members would often ask, "What's happened to you?"

"What do you mean?" I would ask.

"Well, you just *look really good*," they would reply. What they were referring to was a newfound joy and contentment that could not be contained and a zest for life I had not known for years.

Some months later, when witnessing to a young lady one day at work, I described the powerful impact salvation had on my life. "When I was young, growing up in Oklahoma, I loved to wake up early in the morning after a spring rain," I told her. "Everything smelled so fresh and clean, and the birds would sing the most beautiful songs. The world was alive, and I felt as fresh and clean and alive as the world around me.

"Back then I was young and innocent, and the world was a wonderful place," I continued. "Over time, however, after being exposed to one sin and heartache after another, I lost that sense of innocence and no longer enjoyed or appreciated the simple pleasures I had known as a child. But that's what salvation did for me," I told her. "It restored to me the joy and hope I used to have, and I felt clean and innocent all over again. Feelings of failure, disappointment, guilt, hurt and despair were washed away, like after a spring rain. Once again, the world was a beautiful place in which to live, and my life now seemed to have endless possibilities. I actually looked forward to each new day, and I began to say, 'No matter what happens, tomorrow is going to be better than today.' "

The cleansing effect salvation has on a person's soul is described in the Bible in this way:

> *Therefore, if anyone is in Christ, he* [or she] *is a new creation; old things have passed away; behold, all things have become new.*
>
> 2 Corinthians 5:17

That's what Christ promises and delivers—a chance for a change, a change for the better.

Chapter 3

GREATER ILLUMINATION

Therefore, leaving the discussion of the elementary principles of Christ, let us go on to perfection.   Hebrews 6:1

While countless Christian organizations have made notable strides in spreading the Gospel throughout the centuries, many have nonetheless fallen short of understanding or teaching all of what God desires for His children. Just as we want to see our children grow in knowledge and strength, even so God wants to see us, His children, grow in the knowledge of Who He is and the power He has made available to us. Unfortunately, if we rely solely on the teachings of a particular church or denomination, we won't always learn all we need to know about God. Therefore, sometimes it is necessary for God to step in and set things straight, and such was the case in my life immediately following my conversion.

As I have already mentioned, I got saved and baptized in water one Sunday in a little Baptist church, but the Lord had a big surprise in store for me the very next day. That Monday I was meditating on all the things I had experienced throughout the previous eight days. I thought about my recent salvation and decided I needed to become affiliated with a local church. Since I had attended that Baptist church in years past and because I had just experienced the greatest event of my life in that very same place, I thought it only natural that I should start attending services there again on a regular basis. But as I was thinking on this, I heard a voice on the inside of me speak as clearly as I've ever heard anything. It said distinctly, "Don't go back there; they've taught you all they can teach you. I'll teach you now."

Please don't misunderstand or misquote what I'm saying here. I am *not* suggesting that people should leave their church. (If that time ever comes, it will be a decision that must be between them and God.) Nor am I saying that God said the members of that particular congregation were not good people. After all, I knew and loved many of them and owed a great deal to that church for the foundational spiritual truths they had helped establish in my life. I'm just saying that God had much more for me to learn, and it would not be made available in that particular church due to their doctrinal views.

Some people may have an issue with this, but God showed me that making the decision to leave one church or denomination behind in order to pursue a deeper relationship with Him is really no different than what we all desire for our very own children.

When our children have gone as far as they can in public schools, we celebrate the day when they graduate and eventually start attending a "school of higher learning." We don't feel as if the former schools were unimportant or unnecessary. They served their purpose. And we don't feel as if we are betraying the previous instructors or schools in any way because moving on is necessary for our child's progress, and everyone understands and supports that decision for them. They are not just moving on; they are moving up.

In the same way, I didn't feel as if I was being ungrateful for my beloved Baptist church or that I was betraying it by not going back. After all:

1. I was leaving with the fondest of memories and the purest of motives.

2. I was convinced it was God Who was leading me (and He is, after all, the Head of the Church).

3. It would be necessary for me to leave in order to learn everything He wanted me to know (and what I was about to experience was beyond anything I could have ever imagined).

I have learned over the years that God never asks you to leave one thing without offering something much greater down the road, and down the road was exactly where I was headed—literally. Finding more of what God had in store for me meant taking a trip many miles down the highway to visit the home of a very special man who lived in a neighboring state.

Higher Learning

Over the previous few months, I had become acquainted with Preston, Merrell's brother-in-law, a young man from College Station, Texas. On occasion, Preston had made mention of his father, Glenn, but I knew nothing more about Glenn, except that he was a minister. I didn't know his denominational affiliation, nor did I have any knowledge of his doctrinal beliefs. I did know, however, that immediately after

I got saved I had an overwhelming desire to go see him. I was convinced it was an urgency God was putting in my heart, and I told Preston about it. Realizing I had never met his father and that I knew nothing about him personally, Preston responded quite curiously, "But you don't even know him!"

"I know," I acknowledged, "but I know God is dealing with me to go see your dad, so I have to do it."

"All right," Preston agreed. "I guess we need to figure out a way to get down there."

Not possessing much money, and being unemployed at the time, I sold what I could to raise gas money for the trip. Several people heard we were going to Texas and asked if they could come along. To accommodate them, a very dear friend, Julie, borrowed her father's pickup truck with camper, so that we would have plenty of room for everyone who was going.

Preston notified his dad that we would soon be heading his direction, and by the middle of the week we were on our way south to Texas. We had a lot of time to visit during the several hours on the road, and one conversation in particular would prove to play an important role in the events we were about to experience. Preston's wife, Barbara, had been complaining of extreme discomfort throughout the course of the trip. It nearly brought her to the point of tears at times. She explained to me that she had a serious physical condition known as ulcerated colitis. Physicians had delivered to her the tragic news that this condition was incurable, and so Barbara would have to be on medication the rest of her life.

Because of this condition, Barbara's diet would have to be very limited. Even with that precaution, a physician informed her, by the time she was thirty, she would more than likely have to start wearing a colostomy bag. She had been to two different doctors over the last three months, and neither of them had been able to provide her with any relief or hope for the future.

In fact, Barbara had just returned from her last doctor's visit earlier that week and the physician had told her that there was nothing he could do for her. He said the only one that could help her now was God. My heart went out to her. I knew there was nothing I could do to change her situation, but I at least tried to lend a sympathetic ear.

We finally arrived at Brother Glenn's home on Thursday, and he lovingly received us, as if he had always known us. We all sat around, talking and relaxing for a while after the long drive down there, and then Brother Glenn's wife, Alta, said she had something she wanted me to look at.

I went over to the table where she was seated, and she pulled out a large binder, which she said was full of poems that she claimed God had inspired her to write over several years. She directed me to one in particular and said that she felt like God wanted me to read it.

About two months earlier I had taken a trip up to Wyoming with my sister Janet and her husband David. We had camped out in the mountains of the Bridger-Teton National Forest, which was just a few miles from Yellowstone National Park. Each morning I had watched a golden eagle fly out from her nest high on a rocky peak overlooking our campsite. I could hear her chick calling out, until the mother finally returned with some food.

Flowing just a few yards from our tent had been a clear mountain stream filled with brown brook trout, and great herds of elk could be seen at sunrise, literally covering the steep hillsides around us. Now as I looked down at the page before me, there, to my utter astonishment, was a word-by-word description of the very things I had seen during that trip to Wyoming. I thought to myself, "How could this woman have known this about me? We've never met, and we live three hundred and twenty miles apart in different states."

Another thing that got my attention was the woman's name—Alta. That was also my mother's name, and this was (and still is) the only other woman I had ever met personally who had the same first name as my mother.

Later I was to learn that the name Alta meant "high," as in mountains. That is where we get the word *altitude*. Interestingly, God is referred to in the Bible as *"The Most High."* [4] So much was happening in such fine detail that I couldn't simply write it off to chance or coincidence. It appeared that God knew me personally and wanted me to be aware of that fact.

Unbeknownst to us, Brother Glenn held a prayer meeting at his home every Friday night, and we would be able to attend the service. God's timing is always perfect. The next night a small crowd of people showed up and gathered in Brother Glenn's living room. The service finally got started, and the guest ministers, a husband and wife team, rose to their feet to speak. According to Brother Glenn, theses ministers had called him at an earlier date and said they had heard about his Friday night fel-

4. Used 42 times in the New King James Version of the Bible

lowship. They went on to say that they felt like God wanted them to come there and minister. As Brother Glenn explained to me later, his response to them was, "Well, who am I to argue with God? Come on!"

Barbara's Double Blessing

When the wife's turn came, she began to minister in a way I had never witnessed before in the churches back home. At times, she would go around the room and, after pointing out a certain individual, address personal things about them, which she had no natural way of knowing. She would then deliver to that person what she said was a message from God.

The whole time this woman was speaking the air was charged with electricity. I had never felt this before in the churches I had attended, but I was not afraid of it. A sense of awe prevailed in the room, and I was at peace with what was happening.

Barbara had been sitting patiently throughout the service, but her pain level was now becoming unbearable. She leaned over to Preston and whispered quietly, "I can't take this anymore. I have to go lie down." Just as she was preparing to get up and leave the room, the woman who was ministering said, "There is someone here who has colitis. You have been to two different doctors over the last three months, and the last doctor you went to see said the only One who can help you now is God, and he was right. Just receive your healing!" Although she didn't publicly acknowledge it at the time, Barbara told me later that when the woman told her to receive her healing, she suddenly felt a warmth in her abdomen, and all the pain left.

By this time, the woman minister had my full attention. After all, she had just repeated word-for-word the private conversation Barbara and I had on the way to Texas the day before in the camper. She next set her eyes on me and began to tell me things about myself, most of them known by me alone. She also said that I would "receive the 'gift,' as promised." Afterward, her husband spoke for a few minutes, said a brief prayer, and then concluded the meeting.

Barbara rose from her seat and walked over to the visiting female minister. "I'm the person who had colitis," she confessed.

"Yes," the lady minister said, "and there's something else wrong with you in *here*," and she pointed to Barbara's lower abdomen. I knew that Barbara had one son, but I didn't know that she had been told by a staff of seven doctors that she would never be able to bear another child.

The woman continued, "You have a child ... a son, but someone else is raising him ... and has even adopted him. You would like to have another child, but doctors have told you that you can't. You have been heartbroken over this, but God is going to fix that, too, and you will have another son."

The woman reached over and touched Barbara's abdomen, and when she did this Barbara suddenly felt weak all over and staggered backward, slowly crumpling to the floor.

After sitting there on the tile for a few minutes, Barbara gathered her composure and got back up on her feet, apparently all right.

I had been visiting with some of the people after the meeting and then I noticed that the guest lady minister had gone into the dining room. I wanted to meet her, so I thought I would walk over and thank her for coming.

We visited for a few minutes, and while she talked I felt that same electricity as before in the living room, and tears began to well up in my eyes and stream down my face. I excused myself and walked toward the kitchen, to get a paper towel to dry the tears. On the way to the kitchen I walked past a visiting evangelist, who was standing by the dining room table, praying a blessing over

Brother Glenn. When I got beside them, my right hand suddenly went straight up into the air of its own accord, and I spoke out some strange words *"Hadda masada."*

I stood there for a second in that position and then pulled my hand down and looked around to see if anyone had seen or heard what had just happened. I was both embarrassed and perplexed. I didn't understand what had occurred and had no idea what the words were I had just spoken. Nor did I have the slightest clue what they could possibly mean.

One by one all the visitors left Brother Glenn's house, and it was time for us to bed down for the night. Despite all the excitement from the evening's activities, I somehow managed to drift off to sleep.

After a good night's rest, our group had breakfast and then loaded up in the camper truck and headed back north. All the way back to Oklahoma everyone talked about the incredible things they had witnessed in Texas, and many of us were determined to pay a return visit to Brother Glenn's as soon as possible.

Back home, Barbara returned to her physician for a checkup. After running a series of tests, he asked her if she had been seeing another physician.

"No, why?" she answered.

"Because I can't find a trace of the colitis, and you appear to be completely well!" he exclaimed.

Barbara explained that she wouldn't need to come back to see him again because, as she put it, "God healed me at a prayer meeting." Surprisingly, the doctor rejoiced at her testimony, remarking that he also believed in miracles.

Barbara remained pain free from the symptoms of colitis and was able to eat anything she wanted with no ill side effects whatsoever. Then, eighteen months later, she gave birth to a bouncing baby boy they named Jonathan. She called him her "miracle baby."

Interestingly enough, Jonathan is actually a Hebrew word that means, "Yahweh has given" or "gift of God."

Seek and You Will Find

After we had returned home from that trip, I began to seek the meaning of the two strange words I had spoken at Brother Glenn's: *"Hadda masada."* One day, while I was riding in a car with Merrell and another friend, the word *lexicon* came to me. I didn't know what it meant. I asked them if they knew, and one of them answered that they thought it might be a type of dictionary.

Not much longer after that, I ran across a *Strong's* concordance, which contained Greek and Hebrew dictionaries. Thinking that this might provide a solution to the mystery, I searched in the concordance and found that the words I had spoken that night at Brother Glenn's were indeed of ancient origin. *Hadda* is Hebrew for the "stretching forth of the hand," and *masada* is also Hebrew and means a "strong fortress."

I remembered that the lady minister I had met at Brother Glenn's had said that I would *"receive the gift, as promised."* This experience of speaking words in an unknown language must have been what she had been talking about. I also noticed that a similar strange thing had happened to the disciples of Jesus who were gathered for prayer on the Jewish Day of Pentecost in Jerusalem. They all began to speak in languages they had never learned. Peter later explained to other Jews who had witnessed what had taken place:

> *Repent, and let every one of you be baptized in the name of Jesus Christ for the remission of sins; and you SHALL RECEIVE THE GIFT of the Holy Spirit. For THE PROMISE is to you and to your children, and to all*

who are afar off, as many as the Lord our God
will call.   Acts 2:38-39, Emphasis added

Before His death and resurrection, Jesus had fore-
told of this supernatural experience, saying that it
would happen to all those who were true believers:

He who believes and is baptized will be saved;
... And these signs will follow those who believe:
... they will speak with new tongues.
Mark 16:16-17

Jesus didn't say this would happen to a special
select few, but to *"those who believe."*

After my experience, and after spending years
studying the Scriptures and numerous books on the
subject, it became clear to me why I'd had to leave
that Baptist church. God wanted me to experience
everything Christ made available to His Church,
including speaking in tongues. This would not have
been possible if I had stayed in that particular church
because they taught that speaking in tongues was
only for those early disciples. The Scriptures clearly
showed otherwise.

Note again what Acts 2:39 says: *"the promise"* is for
"as many as the Lord our God will call." Nowhere in the

Scriptures can you find that God placed an expiration date on this blessed experience. Unfortunately, most denominations build their doctrines on the scriptural interpretations of their founding fathers. These private interpretations, based primarily on personal opinion, eventually replace or negate some parts of the Bible altogether. How sad!

Jesus denounced a similar practice that went on during His day. He said the religious leaders at that time were, *"Teaching as doctrines the commandments of men"* (Matthew 15:9). The teachings we follow in life need to be founded solely on the Word of God and not on the opinions of man or the traditions of a certain organization. Sadly, many people have made a blind allegiance to a denomination and its beliefs without searching out the Scriptures for themselves, to prove (or disprove) the validity of their leader's or denomination's beliefs.

The apostle Paul said that we should be like the Bereans. They were highly commended because they:

> *... were more fair-minded than those in Thessalonica, in that they ... searched the Scriptures daily to find out whether these things* [they were told] *were so.*   Acts 17:11

As I have said before, I'm not down on Baptists (or any other denomination for that matter), but as my dear Granny used to say, "If the shoe fits, wear it," or, as the popular saying of the day goes, "It is what it is." Simply put, the time has come for the religious leaders of many mainline denominations to admit that they have exalted their traditional views and opinions above the Sacred Scriptures. In the process, they have deprived many sincere and devoted Christians within their ranks of the knowledge they need to experience all the blessings and spiritual authority Jesus made available to them.

Jesus said it very clearly in the book of Matthew:

> *But woe to you, scribes and Pharisees, hypo-crites! For you shut up the kingdom of heaven against men; for you neither go in yourselves, nor do you allow those who are entering to go in.*   Matthew 23:13

George Harrison and Granny's Miracle

So much had happened over the three weeks since my salvation that I was eager to share with others all the extraordinary things I had been experiencing. On one particular night, Merrell and I had been visiting with some people in our neighborhood, discussing the Bible and praying for their needs. I had noticed the sky had an unusual red tint to it all night and had even commented to Merrell that the evening had a strange "feel" to it. The hour eventually grew late, so I went to spend the night with Granny.

When I arrived at Granny's house, I quietly slipped into the spare bedroom, trying my best not to wake her. I had been lying there for only a short time when I decided to say a prayer for Granny's peace of mind. My grandfather had been in the Veteran's Administration Hospital in Oklahoma City for several days undergoing medical treatment for prostate cancer, but after numerous attempts to save him, he had finally succumbed to the disease. It had been less than a week since we had buried him, and my heart went out to Granny.

For as long as I could remember, my grandfather had struggled with alcoholism and would frequently disappear for days at a time. His addiction eventually took its toll on the marriage, resulting in their divorce after decades of having lived together as husband and wife. Despite the heartache he had caused Granny, they had continued to stay in touch over the next several years, and it was obvious to everyone in the family that

Granny still had strong feelings for him when he passed away.

I had seen firsthand over the years how God was faithful to answer a heart-felt, sincere prayer, so I was certain He would answer me now concerning Granny. "Lord," I began. "I ask You to let Granny know You still move in awesome supernatural power, and let her know everything will be all right. And I thank You for it, Amen!" Without giving the prayer a second thought, I settled back in my bed, intent on getting some sleep.

Only a matter of seconds after I had prayed that prayer, however, I began to hear a faint rumbling sound off in the distance to the south. Granny's home was just one block from the railroad tracks, and over the years I had grown accustomed to the distant sound of an approaching train. I figured that must be what I was hearing now and decided not to pay any attention. But as the sound became more distinct, I realized it wasn't coming from the nearby tracks but from the sky. "It must be a jet coming this way," I thought.

The sound kept drawing nearer and nearer, maintaining a steady rumbling and growing in intensity as it got closer. By the time it reached my grandmother's house, the noise had increased to a loud roar, and the instant it was directly over the bedroom, I heard a sudden loud explosion. I was certain the noise was not a sonic boom, since I had heard plenty of them in my early years. Also, by this time, low-flying jets were no longer permitted to pass over cities at supersonic speed. The sound of the explosion soon diminished, and as it rumbled off to the north, I could hear it slowing fading into the distance.

I was lying there trying to understand what had just happened, when I caught the sound of music playing somewhere nearby. I knew there was no radio on anywhere in the house, so I was trying to figure out where the sound was coming from. The open entry to my bedroom allowed a clear view down the hallway to the head of Granny's bed. The music seemed to be coming from her room, and as I glanced in that direction, I noticed a faint light across her bed. I thought to myself, *Where is that light coming from? And what is that music I hear?*

A few months earlier my grandfather had given Granny a portable black-and-white television set. Since she was getting up in years, she had placed the TV on the dresser at the foot of her bed, so that she could watch it as she was lying there.

That, I finally realized, was where the light and music was coming from. The TV must be on.

I lay there listening a little longer to the song and then suddenly recognized the tune. It was a song written by George Harrison entitled, "Here Comes the Sun," which had been recorded by the Beatles on their Abbey Road album. I had been a big fan of the Beatles ever since their first appearance on "The Ed Sullivan Show" back in the mid-1960s. My grandfather had been sitting in the living room with me that night as I watched the Beatles perform on American television for the very first time. I laughed under my breath when he sarcastically compared their long-haired appearance to "a bunch of &^%!#$ sheep dogs!"

I listened now to the music coming from Granny's bedroom. I could only hear the instrumental part of the song, but knowing the song as well as I did, I could mentally follow along with it, filling in the words from memory. These are the words that went with the portion of the song I heard:

> *Little darling, it's been a long cold, lonely winter.*
> *Little darling, it feels like years since it's been here.*

Here comes the sun, here comes the sun.
And I say ...

It was at this point in the song that I actually heard words come from the television for the first time. "It's all right," I heard distinctly. They were the exact words that belonged in that particular part of the song, and as soon as I heard them, the music stopped.

I was trying to absorb everything that had just happened when I heard Granny speak up. "That's funny!" she suddenly exclaimed. "I've seen TVs go off during a storm (supposing the explosion she had just heard was a crash of thunder), but I've never seen one come on in a storm.

"And," she continued, "I just saw the most pleas- ant-looking young man on the screen. I wish I would have had my glasses on, so I could have seen him better. He said something, but I couldn't tell what it was."

"I know what he said," I replied. "He said, 'It's all right.' " I told her the words I had prayed a few minutes earlier and said I believed that God had answered that prayer and was reassuring her that He would be with her, and everything would be all right.

GREATER ILLUMINATION

I got up and went into Granny's room to turn the TV off, but when I looked at the screen, I saw no image at all. All that showed was a snowy white appearance, like it normally had at that time of night. To this day I wonder who (or what) the image was that my grandmother saw on the screen, and I wish I could have seen it myself.

There were several things about this whole incident that got my attention:

- The explosion was specifically in line with what I had prayed about God showing my grandmother that He still moved in "awesome supernatural power."
- There seemed to be no natural explanation for the source of the rumbling sound or the explosion.
- It happened immediately after the prayer for Granny regarding my grandfather's death.
- The TV had been given to her by my grandfather, who had just passed away.
- My grandfather had been watching "The Ed Sullivan Show" with me on another black-and-white TV in that same house in 1964 the first time I had seen the Beatles.

- The song that played that night was one I just happened to know the words to very well because I was a long-time Beatles fan.
- The song had the reassuring message that everything was "all right," exactly in line with what I had just prayed.
- As soon as the words "it's all right" came from the TV, the music stopped, the image disappeared, and the picture went blank.
- The TV had only a rabbit ears antennae, and the few channels we were able to receive did not broadcast programs that late at night.
- The TV actually came on by itself (it had no remote, so it could not have been inadvertently turned on by Granny).

When sharing this story with others, some have expressed curiosity as to why God would use a Beatles song, since the members of that group were not part of a Christian musical group and many times were at the center of public controversy. My answer would be: God used a method of communication with which I was very familiar. I had only recently come out of a life of rock music, and He chose a song, the lyrics and message of which I could readily recognize and one which contained the exact words that provided the precise answer to my prayer.

If I had been more inclined to another style of music that could have conveyed the same message just as well, I believe God would have used that instead. The point is: He is God, and He can use anything He sees fit that gets the job done.

We see examples all throughout the Bible where God used unconventional methods, remarkable circumstances and sometimes questionable people to accomplish His great purposes. Remember, it is not as much about the messenger as it is the message.

We have to be careful about rejecting a gift because we don't like the package it comes in. It appears that the real test of whether or not this was a true act of God is this:

1. Did it bring comfort?
2. Did it glorify God?

I would say "yes" on both counts.

Chapter 4

BATTLING DARK FORCES

For we do not wrestle against flesh and blood,
but against principalities, against powers,
against the rulers of the darkness of this age,
against spiritual hosts of wickedness in the
heavenly places.   Ephesians 6:12

I had already experienced more supernatural events in my life over the last few weeks than I had ever dreamed of, but much more lay ahead in this spiritual school of higher learning that God was taking me through. Only two months had passed since my salvation and the subsequent trip to Brother Glenn's home. I had already come so far in my walk with God, but I still felt as though I knew so very little.

One Sunday afternoon I sensed an urging to consecrate a fast unto the Lord. I started off early Monday morning and continued the fast for five days. During that time, I drank only coffee and water and had only one meal, Wednesday at noon.

Ever since the trip to Brother Glenn's, Merrell and I had been talking about how much we would love to go back and visit him again. So, the last day of my fast (on my 28th birthday), we loaded up and headed back south to the Lone Star State.

Delivered from Evil

We arrived at Brother Glenn's in the evening, just in time for supper. Brother Glenn's wife, Alta, was an excellent cook, and she had prepared a large Mexican meal. As hungry as I was, I was not going to break my fast until God told me I could. I prayed to the Lord and felt assurance that I could now resume a regular diet. I happily grabbed a plate and dug in.

The meal was absolutely delicious, and afterward we went into Brother Glenn's living room to relax. As we sat there, I started up a conversation with Brother Glenn. I told him I had been fasting all week but didn't know why. He replied very confidently, "I do." He said the Lord had told him I would be coming and that I would be needing prayer.

At the time, I didn't know that Brother Glenn had a reputation for boldly confronting the devil. In many

Christian circles, it is known as "the ministry of deliverance." Simply put, deliverance is a supernatural empowerment to set people free from demonic influences that may have held them in bondage to mind-sets, habits and sins for years.

While any Holy Spirit-filled believer is capable of administering deliverance, as the Lord leads, a person who is called to this particular ministry seems to operate more frequently and often on a higher level of power and authority in deliverance than other Christians.

I told Brother Glenn I didn't want anything standing between me and God, and he said he would pray for me. We got up from our chairs and headed toward a room at the back of their house. What happened next is the stuff of Hollywood movies.

While I didn't display any outward weird behavior, such as that shown in the horror movie, "The Exorcist," I did experience something I would never forget. As Brother Glenn began to command any evil spirits to loose their hold on me, I started to feel queasy in my stomach and soon felt something down in my throat slowly moving its way upward. I told Brother Glenn what was happening, and he left the room for a moment, only to return with a large paper bag, which he handed to me. It had some toilet paper loosely folded in the bottom, and he told me to use it to spit up if I felt the need.

Brother Glenn began to pray again, and I felt a small mass moving further up my throat, until it seemed to be lodged near my Adam's apple.

Whatever this thing was, I was not going to let it remain there, so I decided to stick my finger down my throat and cause it to come out. As I gagged myself, I suddenly spit up a clump of something that had a very bitter taste. I spit it out into the paper bag sitting in front of me and then looked down to see what it was. What I saw amazed me. It was a walnut-sized clump that had a black and slimy appearance and reeked of a putrid odor, much like a urinal puts off. I was totally bewildered at what had just taken place but, surprisingly, not afraid at all.

Brother Glenn kept praying a little longer, and after I spit up a little more of the slimy substance, the deliverance session was over. Later I asked Brother Glenn what had happened. I had just eaten a large Mexican meal only minutes before the deliverance, and yet I had not thrown up any food at all. This meant that the slimy substance, whatever it was, hadn't come from my stomach. And, if it didn't come from my stomach, then where did it come from? And what exactly was it?

Brother Glenn referred to the substance I spit up as "the gall of bitterness." Throughout the course of our lives we have numerous opportunities to become bitter due to broken promises, disappointments, abandonment and betrayal. Brother Glenn said he thought this mass was simply bitterness that had accumulated inside of me over time.

As to where it came from, Brother Glenn agreed that it did not come from my stomach, but obviously it came from somewhere inside my body. He said he thought it could have lodged itself somewhere in or around my organs, and the prayer of authority used during the deliverance session had caused it to dislodge and come out. He also said he believed that bitterness unchecked and unresolved can eventually develop into some types of disease, such as cancer.

After the deliverance session, I also understood why God had led me to fast all week. We all know from experience how some natural things in our life are harder to get rid of than others, whether they be bad habits or excess weight. Some simply take more effort or require more extreme measures before we're successful at overcoming them.

This applies to spiritual things, too. There is an account in Matthew that gives us more insight into the principles of dealing with the evil spirits who oppress humans. In this passage, Jesus had commanded His disciples to go preach the Gospel, heal the sick and cast out demons. They had been very successful in dealing with demons, but on one particular occasion, try as they might, the disciples could not cast a demon out of a young man who was plagued with epileptic seizures. When the disciples asked Jesus what had prevented them from setting the boy free, He responded:

> ... *this kind does not go out except by prayer and fasting.* Matthew 17:21

My deliverance had taken place on the evening of my 28th birthday, and I just couldn't have imagined a better birthday present. But God was not through giving me His heavenly gifts yet. An even more glorious supernatural experience lay just around the corner.

Spiritual Conflict

The next morning was a beautiful Saturday, so Merrell and I decided to take a walk down a winding road in Brother Glenn's neighborhood. After a brief stroll, we made our way back to his house. Brother

BATTLING DARK FORCES

Glenn had a beautiful Irish Setter, and when we arrived back at his property, the dog was sitting in the middle of the entrance to the driveway that led up to the house. We walked up to the dog and patted it on the head, but when we attempted to walk around it and enter the property, the dog got up, walked over in front of us, and sat down again. This happened two more times, until we became somewhat annoyed with the dog's actions.

Speaking firmly to the dog, we said, "Move!" Then the dog got up and trotted off down the road away from the house. Despite our attempts to call it back to the yard, it proceeded on down the road and disappeared around a bend.

We were a little puzzled by what had just happened, and we made our way to the house to tell Brother Glenn about his dog. To our surprise, as we entered the house we saw Brother Glenn's Irish Setter lying on the floor in the den. We were rather confused and told Brother Glenn what had just occurred.

"Yes, I know," he replied. "That dog is from a house down the road, and he has an unclean spirit. He didn't want you on the property, and he was afraid to come in himself." That was our first direct contact with a creature being used by the enemy, but it would not be our last. That very evening we were to have yet another unwelcome visitor.

Trampling on the Enemy

We had a wonderful time of fellowship with Brother Glenn and his family that day, but when evening came, we were ready to catch some shut-eye. Merrell and I were just like brothers, so we didn't mind when we were told we would both have to sleep in the spare room.

Merrell was lying across a bed reading his Bible, and I was seated in a chair, taking my shoes off, when I spied some movement out of the corner of my eye. As I looked down at the carpet, just to my right, I saw a scorpion headed straight for the bed Merrell was on. When it got about three feet away, it suddenly stopped and flipped over on its back.

For a while, the creature showed no sign of movement, so I wondered if it had somehow suddenly died. I pointed the scorpion out to Merrell, and he said, "That's really weird. Listen to the scripture I was just reading in Luke 10:"

BATTLING DARK FORCES

Behold, I give you the authority to trample on serpents and SCORPIONS, and over all the power of the enemy, and nothing shall by any means hurt you.

Luke 10:19, Emphasis added

I thought it was very unusual that Merrell had been reading that exact scripture at that moment, but I considered the scorpion's behavior equally unusual. I walked over to where the scorpion was lying and, after picking up a stick, I poked it gently in the abdomen. No sooner had I touched the scorpion than it responded by rapidly thrusting out its tail and striking the stick with its stinger. The scorpion was obviously very much alive, but I still couldn't understand why it had acted in such a peculiar way. It was almost as if it reached an invisible barrier, which prevented it from coming any closer to the bed, and the moment it did, something flipped it over on its back and immobilized it.

When I saw it strike the stick, I took to heart the scripture Merrell had just quoted and used my shoe to *"trample"* on the scorpion. When I was satisfied that it was no longer a threat, I finished getting ready for bed and turned out the light.

A Heavenly Language

The next morning Merrell and I got up, and I decided to take a shower and freshen up before breakfast. When I walked out of the bathroom, Brother Glenn was seated in his armchair in the living room, watching a Dallas Cowboys football game on TV. The last time I had been to his home, I had spoken those two words in the Hebrew language, *"Hadda masada."* Although I was almost certain I had experienced what the Bible refers to as "speaking in tongues," I had not spoken any more unusual words like that since.

One of the key tactics the devil uses to prevent you from moving forward in the things of God is to place doubt in our mind, especially after a notable spiritual experience. He did the same thing to Jesus after He had been baptized by John in the Jordan river.

In Luke 4, we find this dialogue between Satan and Christ:

Then Jesus, being filled with the Holy Spirit, returned from the Jordan and was led by the Spirit into the wilderness, being tempted for forty days by the devil. And in those days He ate nothing, and afterward, when they had ended, He was very hungry. And the devil said to Him, "IF You are the Son of God, command this stone to become bread."   Luke 4:1-3, Emphasis added

You will notice that the first word Satan used was *if*. That was a word of doubt. Satan will always try to get you to question your relationship with God and the reliability of His Word. True to his nature, the devil had been filling my mind with thoughts of doubt over the last few weeks, and I just had to know for sure whether I had actually received the gift of the Holy Spirit and whether or not I had spoken with new tongues. So, I decided to bring this matter up with Brother Glenn and settle the issue once and for all.

I walked over to where he was sitting in an arm chair and knelt down on one knee beside him. I explained to him what was on my heart, and without any hesitation, he spoke a very simple, yet powerful, prayer. "Father, ..." he began. At the moment he said the word *Father*, I felt a wave of intense electricity start at the top of my head and sweep down the full length of my body.

"You see my brother," Brother Glenn continued. When he finished saying those words I felt a second wave of electricity rush down my body. "I ask You to help him to know that he knows he has the Holy Ghost, so he'll never doubt it again," he prayed. No sooner had he finished praying those last words than a third and more powerful surge of electricity hit my body. Then Brother Glenn reached over and gently touched my forehead with the fingertips of his right hand. When he did, I suddenly sprang to my feet, threw my arms straight up and turned my face heavenward with my eyes closed. At the exact same moment, a stream of unknown words exploded from deep within me, and I was crying out at the top of my voice.

I spoke those strange words for what seemed to be several minutes, but was probably only about thirty seconds. The whole time I was speaking I could see a mental image of God sitting on a large throne and could sense His great love for me, and tears of joy streamed down my face.

I soon became overly conscious of what I was doing, and the language slowly died down. I lowered my arms and sat down on the floor. Brother Glenn's daughter had also been seated in the room when all of this happened, and I later asked her what the language I had spoken sounded like. She worked in an office through the week, at Texas A&M University, and was exposed to many people from many different foreign countries. "Well, I don't know for sure," she started.

"But it sounded to me like fluent Russian, and it sounded like you had been speaking it all your life."

After reflecting back on this situation over the years, I have learned a few things. You will remember I had just undergone deliverance only two nights before, and I had asked God to remove anything that stood between me and Him. I am convinced that there can be things within us that block the full flow of God's Spirit, much like a hose that is plugged up and allows only a trickle of water to pass through. When the blockage is removed, water can gush forth freely, and I believe that is what happened on that Sunday morning in Brother Glenn's living room. Now I would never doubt again.

Just as the disciples in Acts 2, I had truly been filled with the Holy Spirit:

> *And they were all filled with the Holy Spirit and began to speak with other tongues, as the Spirit gave them utterance.* Acts 2:4

Power Over Spirits

As much as we hated to leave Brother Glenn's, it was time for Merrell and me to go back home and resume our normal routines. When we were just pulling back into our town, I decided to run by one of the local convenience stores and put some gas in the car. As we sat there, the Holy Spirit suddenly spoke to me in a rapid-fire manner saying, "Sharon [an old girlfriend] is about to pull up in her car. She has been drinking [alcohol] and will ask you to go with her to her house. It's all right. It's of Me, so tell her yes." I was so certain that what I had heard was from God that I quickly told Merrell about it.

No sooner had I spoken these words to Merrell than Sharon came wheeling around the corner and pulled up beside us. From her loud, slurred speech, it was obvious that she was intoxicated. We talked for a few minutes, and then she asked us to come over to her house. She said she needed to run into the store first to get some more beer and said she would meet us at her house in a few minutes. Normally I wouldn't have wanted to be around someone who was drinking, but since the Holy Spirit had told me it was all right, I knew something good would come of it. So we agreed.

As we left the store, I felt an urgency to get to Sharon's house before she did, even though I didn't know why. We sped over to her mobile home and pulled into the yard, and I jumped out of my car, carrying a Bible in my right hand.

BATTLING DARK FORCES

As I approached Sharon's house my right hand suddenly shot up into the air of its own volition, pointing toward a spot a few feet over the roof of the house. At the same time my hand went up, to my total surprise, strong words of rebuke sprang out of my mouth. "You governing spirits," I heard myself say, "I command you to leave in the name of Jesus!"

No sooner had I spoken those words of authority than I heard the sound of two very large hogs grunting behind us about two blocks away to the east. The size of most animals can be easily determined by the sound they make. For example, a Chihuahua is recognizable by its weaker, high-pitched, yapping sound, while a Saint Bernard is distinguished by its stronger, low-pitched, woofing sound. Judging by these standards, and given the fact that I had been raised around a rural community and had seen my fair share of swine, I concluded that the hogs we had heard were much larger than any I had ever seen. In fact, I estimated that each of them had to be about as big as a Volkswagen van.

I'm aware of the fact there are no actual physical swine that large on earth, but what I believe we encountered that night was not creatures of this natural world at all, so normal rules would not have applied in this case.

After hearing the grunting sounds, Merrell glanced over at me and, with a look of surprise on his face, asked, "Did you hear that?"

Wanting to be sure we had just experienced the same thing, I asked, "Hear what?"

He exclaimed, "It sounded like two giant hogs!"

I replied in a very serious tone, "Yes, I did hear them."

Merrell had been around plenty of livestock himself and knew of a certainty that what we had heard was absolutely not normal.

About that time Sharon came around the corner and pulled up in the yard. She got out of her car and opened the door of the trailer to let us in. It was after dark, so she turned on the porch light. As soon as she flipped the switch, the light blinked twice. Merrell and I thought it significant that we had just heard two hogs, and that light had blinked two times.

We spent the rest of the evening fellowshipping over the things of God, instead of drinking beer as Sharon had hoped and planned. In addition, Merrell felt led to lay hands on and pray for her young son, who had been extremely ill for quite some time. God wonderfully touched the boy, and he quickly recovered that night, much to the amazement and extreme delight of his mother.

BATTLING DARK FORCES

The next day I sensed the Lord speaking to me that if we would take a drive back over to Sharon's neighborhood and go to the general area from where we had heard the grunting sounds, He would teach us some things about what had happened the night before. I shared this with Merrell, and we loaded up in my car and headed in that direction.

We drove past Sharon's house and arrived at the place where we had heard the hogs. The area was located next to a Kingdom Hall of Jehovah's Witnesses. Next door to the hall was a livestock corral, and I pulled the car over beside that corral and got out to look around. I noticed an elderly man in the corral feeding some horses and asked him if this place had always been used as a corral. Interestingly, he said that many years before a man had raised hogs in that same location. That really got my attention.

I could have written his comment off as a strange coincidence, but the information he volunteered next set me back on my heels. "And you know," he continued, "I don't know if it's true, but I heard that years ago, before white people settled this area, Indian medicine men would gather on this spot and conjure up spirits." You should have seen the look on Merrell's face when he heard that. It wasn't hard for either of us to put two and two together. I was certain that this was exactly what God had sent us over there to find out.

As I have noted, God always confirms to us that He is leading us so that we don't write off what we hear Him saying as imagination or mere coincidence. Hogs ... evil spirits ... it all just fell perfectly into place.

I thought this was all that God had to teach us about this encounter, but I couldn't have been more mistaken. The fact that these hogs sounded very large seemed to be indicative of their level of strength. These were no small imps we had heard, but, rather, demons of a ruling class. The words I had spoken at Sharon's house that night now seemed to make perfect sense. "Governing spirits" aptly described the nature of these entities.

Symbolically, hogs in the Bible are always connected with evil, unclean spirits. In the book of Mark, we find the account of the madman of Gadara who was possessed. When Jesus commanded the spirits to come out of the man, they begged Jesus to allow them to enter a herd of swine that was grazing nearby. Jesus told them to "go," and they entered the swine and destroyed them:

BATTLING DARK FORCES

*Then the unclean spirits went out and entered
the swine (there were about two thousand); and
the herd ran violently down the steep place into
the sea, and drowned in the sea.* Mark 5:13

What Merrell and I learned next seemed to paint
a clearer picture of what evil plans the devil had in
store for Sharon and why God had arranged for me
to arrive at her house ahead of her. A little later that
day we heard from a close friend that the man who
lived directly behind Sharon had died from alcoholism the night before we heard the hogs.

We have seen from the account of the madman of
Gadara that when evil spirits leave a person they
want to enter into something or, preferably, someone else. Jesus explained more on the subject, when
He said:

*When an unclean spirit goes out of a man, he
goes through dry places, seeking rest; and finding none, he says, "I will return to my house
from which I came."* Luke 11:24

We have already established through scripture
that evil spirits prefer to inhabit a living being as
opposed to remaining outside of one, and this is

how God explained to me what unfolded that night we heard the large hogs. The man next door to Sharon had just died and had died from alcoholism. So, in essence, he drank himself to death (which is a form of suicide, or taking of his own life, similar to the pigs in the Bible who ran into the sea and drowned themselves). In the case of the pigs, they were destroyed instantly, while the man poisoned himself over a period of time. What he had at work in his life were two controlling, or governing spirits—suicide and alcoholism.

At the time this happened, many people had expressed a concern about Sharon becoming an alcoholic because she had begun to drink heavily and frequently, a destructive habit that seemed to run in her family. The Lord showed me that after the man living behind her died, true to scripture, the spirits left him and began to seek out another living body to inhabit. Because of her vulnerability, Sharon would have made an easy target. That was why I had felt such an urgency in my spirit that night to make it to her house before she did. Those two spirits had just vacated their former "house" and were waiting at that moment to spiritually ambush Sharon as soon as she got home. Thank God He had other plans for her.

What God did for Sharon is so typical of Him. At our weakest moments, when we are incapable of helping ourselves, out of His love and mercy, He sends someone or some situation along to help us.

It is worthy of note here that I was a relatively recent convert at this time, yet God used me to battle against the forces of darkness for Sharon's sake. Although I was fairly new in the things of the Lord, as a Christian, I still had God's Spirit residing within me, and that was the power which overcame those ruling demons that night.

God expressed it this way through Zechariah:

> *"Not by might nor by power* [of man], *but by My Spirit,"*
> *Says the Lord of hosts.*   Zechariah 4:6

Before He ascended to Heaven, Jesus told His followers that this authority over the forces of darkness would be granted to all those who believed in Him, not just the twelve apostles, as many believe:

> *And He said to them, "Go into all the world and preach the gospel to every creature. He who believes and is baptized will be saved; but he who does not believe will be condemned. And these signs will follow those who believe: In My name they will cast out demons."*   Mark 16:15-17

It is vital to notice what Jesus said here in Mark, that *"these signs WILL* [not maybe] *follow those* [meaning anyone and everyone] *who believe."* Are you a believer, one who has been saved and baptized into Christ? If so, then this set of scriptures says that you, too, have been given that authority. You can do something similar to what I did, if the Lord leads you in that direction.

Satan does not want humanity to know what power has been provided to the Body of Christ, and one of the more subtle ways he does this is to fool us into believing that this authority was only made available to the early church and only to a select few. This doctrinal error has infiltrated many mainline denominations, and the end result has been a weak, defeated, ineffective church. Sure, leaders of these churches may preach and teach the message of salvation and God's love, but their converts still end up living far below the authority and privileges they have available to them, and they teach others to do the same.

Speaking of Jesus, the Bible says:

> *For this purpose the Son of God was manifested,*
> *that He might destroy the works of the devil.*
> 1 John 3:8

BATTLING DARK FORCES

When Jesus left the earth, He planned for this ministry of destroying the works of the devil to continue. The responsibility of carrying on this type of spiritual warfare was passed on to His believers throughout all generations. Jesus explained it this way:

> *Most assuredly, I say to you, he* [anyone] *who believes in Me, the works that I do he will do also; and greater works than these he will do, because I go to my Father. And whatever you ask in My name, that I will do, that the Father may be glorified in the Son.*   John 14:12-13

God is always expanding our knowledge and understanding, and during the writing of this book He added yet another confirmation to what had happened at Sharon's house. When I rebuked the demons that night, the words *governing spirits* came out of my mouth. Although I was confident they came from God, I wondered for years about that particular choice of words. Then, in 2013, I ran across a book by Kenneth E. Hagin entitled, *The Triumphant Church: Dominion over all the Powers of Darkness.* [5] In chapter 6, "How to Deal with Evil Spirits," Rev.

5. Tulsa, Oklahoma (Kenneth Hagin Ministries: 1993)

97

Hagin said that Jesus appeared in a vision and spoke to him at length concerning the operation of demons in people's lives. He went on to say that the Lord explained to him that the spirits which controlled the madman of Gadara were actually *"governing"* the man. This new information seemed to put a cap on the experience I had that night at Sharon's house.

It is also crucial to note that I had not planned or chosen to confront those demons. The entire event was totally orchestrated by God. It was His Spirit through me which rose up at that moment and drove the demons from Sharon's house.

If God had told me what I was to do ahead of time, I might have been hesitant to attempt it. If we step out on our own to confront the forces of darkness, without the leading of God or the empowerment of His Spirit, disastrous results can follow. Just look at the following account from the Acts of the Apostles:

> *Now God worked unusual miracles by the hands of Paul, so that even handkerchiefs or aprons were brought from his body to the sick, and the diseases left them and the evil spirits went out of them. Then some of the itinerant Jewish exorcists TOOK IT UPON THEM-*

SELVES to call the name of the Lord Jesus over those who had evil spirits, saying, "We exorcise you by the Jesus whom Paul preaches." Also there were seven sons of Sceva, a Jewish chief priest, who did so.

And the evil spirit answered and said, "Jesus I know, and Paul I know; but who are you?"

Then the man in whom the evil spirit was leaped on them, overpowered them, and prevailed against them, so that they fled out of that house naked and wounded. This became known both to all Jews and Greeks dwelling in Ephesus; and fear fell on them all, and the name of the Lord Jesus was magnified.

Acts 19:11-17, Emphasis added

Free Indeed

I had learned a great deal about demon activity through this experience with Sharon, and I was soon to gain more understanding of how demons had influenced my own life. There's an old saying, "You don't know what you have until it's gone," and this proved true for me in my experience with deliverance. I had dated a girl for quite some time before my salvation, and we had our fair share of arguments and misunderstanding. I knew I harbored some hard feelings toward her, but I always did my best to be friendly when we met. I had noticed, however, that every time I would see her out in public, I would get a slight queasy feeling in my stomach (similar to what I felt at the beginning of my deliverance). Then, several days after I underwent my deliverance session with Brother Glenn, I saw her at a local restaurant back in my hometown. I sat down at a table by myself to look over the menu, and I suddenly noticed that when I looked her way that old familiar, uncomfortable feeling in my gut was gone.

Then I understood. I had allowed that "gall of bitterness" Brother Glenn had spoken about to creep into my soul in the form of resentment and unforgiveness, which brought on the queasiness I felt. Since I had submitted myself to deliverance, the source of that queasiness was gone. Jesus said:

> *Therefore if the Son makes you free, you shall*
> *be free indeed.*   John 8:36

It was by the Holy Spirit's power working through Brother Glenn that I had been set free from the demonic influence that made me feel bitter toward her.

Chapter 5

A HEART ON FIRE

Who makes ... His ministers flames of fire.
Hebrews 1:7

The Lord had taught me many spiritual truths since my initial salvation and introduced me to several new experiences along the way. I now had a burning desire to share these truths and experiences with others, so that they could walk in the same freedom and power and feel the same joy I had come to know. There was an excitement inside that I truly could not contain.

Jeremiah, an Old Testament prophet, felt a similar passion burning within when he said:

> *But His word was is in my heart like a burning fire,*
> *Shut up in my bones;*
> *I was weary of holding it back,*
> *And I could not.*   Jeremiah 20:9

Everywhere I went I testified of the wonderful things God had done for me, and I shared from the Scriptures the liberating truths He had revealed. Although I did run across a few doubters and skeptics, most of the people I encountered received me with open arms and listened with interest as I poured out my heart and soul.

I began by speaking to close friends and family members, but it wasn't long before I was witnessing to casual acquaintances and total strangers as well.

I have come to see that God wants the whole world to know about Him, and He will provide you with plenty of opportunities to share His love and His Word. Even when you encounter what appears to be a roadblock, God will intervene and make a way, proving true to His Word as found in Revelations 3:8:

> *I know your works. See, I have set before you an open door, and no one can shut it.*
>
> Revelation 3:8

One roadblock I ran up against involved a close friend I wanted to visit who was battling a fatal form of cancer. He was hospitalized in Oklahoma City, and because of the seriousness of his condition, the only people allowed in his room were close family members and licensed clergy. While I had some remarkable testimonies to share of God's love and power and a decent working knowledge of the Scriptures from which to preach and teach, I didn't possess credentials from a recognized ministry that would allow me entrance into many places.

I continued to witness wherever I could, but I now saw the genuine need to become a licensed minister. Since I didn't have the money at the time to attend a seminary or Bible college but continued to run across people who needed ministry, I prayed that God would make a special way for me to obtain a license and quickly. The opportunity came directly following that prayer, and it happened in the most unexpected way.

Bud Chambers and Open Doors

Merrell and I had known about the evangelistic ministry of Reverend Bud Chambers for several years, and one day we decided to attend one of the evening services held at his church in Oklahoma City. The songs were very uplifting that night, and following the service we decided to walk up to the platform and tell Rev. Chambers how much we had enjoyed the service.

After a few moments, Rev. Chambers asked us where we were from, and we told him Pauls Valley, which was about fifty miles away. "Well," he said, "I was just getting ready to go to a restaurant and have some coffee and grab a bite to eat. I know it's kind of late and you have a long drive home, but I would like for you to join me." Merrell and I considered it a privilege to be able to visit with this well-respected minister on a more personal level, so we were more than happy to take him up on his offer.

Once we made it to the restaurant, we ordered some coffee and became engaged in some casual conversation, but it wasn't long before Rev. Chambers said something that both pleased and surprised us. "I know we just met, and I wouldn't normally do this, but I really feel impressed of the Lord to provide you two with a ministerial license through my evangelistic association."

There had been many moments up to that time in which both Merrell and I had seen the need to minister but couldn't, and now, thanks to Brother Chambers, we would have an open door that would enable us to reach out to many more. We thanked this man of God for his kind and generous offer and told him we knew it was all arranged by God because it was a direct answer to a recent prayer.

After the meal, we followed Rev. Chambers back
to his church, where he presented us both with a
card stating we were now licensed ministers in good
standing with the Bud Chambers Evangelistic Association. Merrell and I were thrilled to finally be
licensed ministers and excited about the new opportunities this would make available.

Thanks to Rev. Chambers, over the next several
months, we were able to minister to a larger number of people, including those in hospitals, jails and
nursing homes, and we even officiated at a few fu-
nerals and weddings.

The Works of Jesus

Merrell and I loved sharing the Gospel with others,
and one particular evening we decided to visit some
people in our neighborhood. It was a wonderful
evening of fellowship with friends in the neighborhood, but then it was getting late, and I decided to
call it a night. After arriving home, I headed to the
bathroom to go though my usual hygiene regiment
before retiring to bed.

After brushing my teeth, I washed my face. As I
was drying off my neck, I felt a lump underneath
the hand towel. When I lifted the cloth, I saw what

appeared to be a growth beneath the skin about the size of a large grape. It had no discoloration and I felt no pain from it, but it was obviously abnormal.

Instead of being gripped with fear, a sudden surge of anger came over me, and I quickly placed my right hand on the lump. I was in the process of saying, "You foul lump, I command you to leave me now, in Jesus' name," but I barely got the first two words out of my mouth when I suddenly heard a "bloop" sound and the lump instantly disappeared.

Afterward, this whole episode seemed surprising to me in many ways. First of all, I didn't know when the lump had first formed. Secondly, I didn't know what it actually was. Thirdly, and the most perplexing of all, I was amazed that the lump went away before I could get the whole sentence out or even speak Jesus' name.

Sometime later I was reading the story in the 9th chapter of Acts where the apostle Peter had prayed for a woman named Tabitha, who had become sick and died. The Scriptures record:

And turning to the body, he [Peter] *said, "Tabitha, arise." And she opened her eyes, and when she saw Peter she sat up.* Acts 9:40

I noticed here that Peter had not used the name of Jesus. Rather, he had simply exercised the authority Christ had given to the disciples when He told them:

Most assuredly, I say to you, he who believes in Me, the works that I do he will do also.

John 14:12

Further along, in John 17, after praying for His disciples, Jesus prayed to the Father regarding everyone else who would ever believe in Him for generations to come:

I do not pray for these alone, but also for those who will believe in Me through their word; that they all may be one, as You, Father, are in Me, and I in You; that they also may be one in Us, that the world may believe that You sent Me. And the glory which You gave Me I have given them, that they may be one just as We are one: I in them, and You in Me. John 17:20-23

Jesus drew spiritual power from His union with God, and we, through our union with Christ, have been granted access to that same mighty power, a power which enables us to do the same works Jesus did. As evidenced in my own life, when we abide in Christ and His Words abide in us, we are capable of operating on an especially high level of faith and authority that brings instant and incredible results.

God's Employment Agency

Ever since my salvation, I had been spending all my time studying God's Word, reading books by Christian authors, attending revivals and seminars, testifying of God's goodness and power, and praying for everyone I could. But one day, as I was studying the Bible, I felt the Lord clearly speak to me that it was time for me to get a secular job. I didn't know where to look, so I simply asked Him to show me where He wanted me to go. In less than thirty minutes I saw Jimmy, a minister friend, pull up in front of my house. He got out of his car and walked up to the front door, and I invited him in.

Jimmy said, "I can't stay long, but I just found out about a job opening here in town, and I wanted to come over right away and tell you about it. I don't even know if you're looking for a job or not, but I just felt like I was supposed to come over here and tell you about this." I told him what the Lord had spoken to me just minutes earlier and said I believed he was being used of God to help provide me the job I was supposed to have. Jimmy was excited to know he had actually heard from God and said he would pray that I get the position.

The opening was at a meat market that was located several blocks across town. Since I didn't have a car, I knew it would take some time to get there, so I immediately started out walking.

Once I arrived at the market, I told the owner why I had come. We had a brief visit and, even though I had no previous experience working in a meat market, he offered me the job. I eagerly started to work early the next day and began to learn the ins and outs of the butcher trade.

Secrets of the Heart

The owner had two other people working in his store, one of which was a young lady who seemed to be shy and spoke very little. I know that some people are just naturally quiet, but I sensed this young woman had many things troubling her. I was convinced she needed a closer relationship with God, and over the next few days I would bring up the Bible whenever I could.

One day I felt impressed to share with this young lady some of the supernatural aspects of God I had learned over the last several months. I told her that God loved her and knew everything about her life. I also began to explain about the word of knowledge as mentioned in 1 Corinthians 12:8. This is a gift of the Holy Spirit whereby God supernaturally reveals to a Christian secrets of the heart about someone else's life. The young lady said she had never heard of such a thing and, furthermore, she didn't believe in it.

I told her that God is a gentleman and wouldn't impose on her privacy, but if she would give Him permission, then He would show me something personal about her.

She responded, "Sure, go ahead," obviously not convinced that anything at all would happen. I prayed out loud that God would reveal something to me about her, thanked Him, and then went back to work.

As I stood there processing meat that day, the words *pink poodle* came to me. I turned to her and said, "Have you ever had a pink poodle?" When she came back with a firm, "no," I was a little puzzled because I was certain I had heard those words clearly.

Suddenly the words *she's lying* came to me. Now I *knew* I had heard clearly and that the words were accurate, so I asked her once again, "Are you sure you've never had a pink poodle?"

This time she looked as if she was searching back somewhere in her memory, and then she said, "Wait a minute! I remember now. I *did* have a pink poodle when I was very young." She went on to tell me a long story about how much she loved that dog and how sad she had been the day she lost it. It seemed to me highly unlikely that she had actually forgotten about that dog. She probably simply didn't want to acknowledge the fact that God did know something personal about her.

Many people find that thought unsettling because of the kind of life they have lived and the mistakes they've made, but God is one Person whom you can trust with your secrets, failures and disappointments, as well as your hopes and dreams.

God went on to reveal some other things to me, including the lady's sister's given name and nickname. Whether or not she accepted my explanation for it all, she certainly knew that something remarkable had happened that day, something that she couldn't afford to ignore.

Lightning Strikes

I loved sharing the Word of God with others, especially with friends I had known for years. I was well acquainted with their families and, despite the fact that many of them had a rather rough veneer, I would often see a tender heart peeking through. One such person was Lonnie.

Lonnie had been raised around a home where liquor and bars were the order of the day, so he had naturally followed suite and began drinking at an early age. Eventually, he had also started taking drugs. But, regardless of his unsavory habits, Lonnie was a very likeable person, and I saw a kind soul inside of him. God had delivered me from a destructive lifestyle of drugs and alcohol, and I wanted Lonnie to experience the same kind of freedom I had come to know.

Lonnie was always willing to talk about God, and one night he invited me over to his house to have dinner and discuss some things about the Bible. We had a great night of fellowship, and I shared many scriptures with Lonnie about God's forgiveness, love and power.

Despite his appreciation of the Bible and his obvious thirst for more knowledge of the Scriptures,

A HEART ON FIRE

Lonnie had not yet fully surrendered his life to God. I left his house that night with a burden in my heart for him to draw closer to God.

I had now done all that I could through witnessing and testifying of what God had done for me, and I knew that only God could affect a total change in Lonnie's heart. Lonnie could be very stubborn, and I somehow believed that it would take something dramatic to get through to him. Before I went home that night, I prayed that God would reveal His power to Lonnie in an unmistakable way.

A couple of days later I saw Lonnie again. I told him what I had prayed, and he said God had answered it. I asked him what he meant, and he said that after I had left that night he was sitting in his living room, talking to God and wondering if God really heard his prayers, when suddenly there was a bright light and a loud noise. A bolt of lightning had struck a tree in his front yard just outside the living room. He had not been expecting such a powerful display, but now, he said, he no longer doubted God.

I'm not saying that God will always speak in such an extraordinary way, of course. Nor am I suggesting we should ask for it. What I *am* saying is that it is not unheard of for God to use awesome displays of the forces of nature to make His power and presence known, as we see recorded in the Old Testament passage:

> *... and the L*ORD *sent thunder and hail, and fire darted to the ground.*   Exodus 9:23

Chapter 6

INTO THE SHADOWS

Do not be unequally yoked together with unbelievers. For what fellowship has righteousness with lawlessness? Or what communion has light with darkness? 2 Corinthians 6:14

God had brought me a long way and showed me many marvelous things, and I would like to say that I stayed on the straight and narrow path, never veering to the right or left, but that just wasn't the case. Over the next several months I began a gradual descent into darkness, which I hadn't planned or expected. I soon learned the hard way that we open ourselves up to Satan's attack when we let our guard down.

I have heard it said, "The road to Hell is paved with good intentions," and I certainly was operating off of good intentions when I began to unknowingly set myself up for failure.

When I had first gotten saved, I was not attending services regularly at any church because I didn't know of a church anywhere near my home that taught or practiced the things I had come to understand and was experiencing. Consequently, I didn't fellowship with very many Christians.

Instead, I spent a lot of time with old friends. I didn't see a problem with this since I always talked to my friends about God and never participated in any of their bad habits. When, on rare occasions, things did begin to get out of hand, I always excused myself and left.

I honestly felt no temptation around these friends and always strived to keep my spiritual strength built up by constantly praying and feeding on the Word of God. I remember attending a party where alcohol was being served, and before long several people were sitting with me around a table discussing God and the Bible.

To me, it seemed as if I was getting the upper hand over the devil, and I had high hopes of winning many of my old friends over to the Kingdom of God. Instead, Satan was slowly, meticulously setting me up for defeat.

Satan is shown to be the deceiver of *"the whole world"* in Revelation 12:9 and I didn't realize that he was fooling me into believing I would never be affected by hanging out with my old friends. The Bible warns us in 1 Corinthians 15:33: *"Do not be deceived: evil company*

116

corrupts good manners." Sure enough, my soul was slowly being corrupted by the worldly influence I was being exposed to.

The King James Version of Genesis 3:1 describes Satan's characteristics this way: *"He was more subtle than any beast of the field,"* meaning that he was the most crafty and cunning of all. True to his nature, Satan was steadily weakening my resistance to sin without me even being aware of it.

The Prodigal Path

Everything suddenly fell apart one night when I was spending time with my two closest buddies. We had been to Oklahoma City to visit some mutual friends and listen to a band, when I made a foolish mistake that sent my life into a downhill plunge.

We had started back home, and as soon as we got on the road, one of my friends pulled out a joint of marijuana and promptly lit it up. I was sitting in the back seat, and at first didn't give it a second thought. I had been around people smoking pot since I had been saved and had easily turned down numerous offers. Unlike many former smokers, who fiercely battled the urge, smelling the odor of marijuana had never given me the desire to try it again. For some reason, this time was different.

One of my friends took a puff and then turned around to me and said, "You want a hit? Just one won't hurt you." I knew better, but I accepted his offer and took one drag off of the joint. Immediately I felt something change. I can't recall exactly the order of the steps, but all I can say is that before I knew it I was back doing all the things I used to do. I found myself once again smoking pot, drinking and going to all the same old places.

I did notice something very unusual though. Now it took me more liquor to get the same high I used to get before I was saved, and now I didn't get the same satisfaction out of smoking pot that I had before.

A Sharp Rebuke

Of course, I no longer felt the joy I had when I was living for God, but the most unpleasant thing that I experienced after I backslid was a conversation I had with a man who had been one of my best friends for years. I had walked into a local bar to grab a cold beer and look for some running buddies, when I saw David sitting in a booth. David and I had been close friends for most of my life, and I was glad to see him. I greeted him and sat down with him, but what he said next floored me.

Instead of smiling at me and greeting me warmly, like usual, David frowned and spoke these cutting words: "What are you doing in here? You know, when I heard that you got saved, I had a little hope. I knew what kind of sinful life you had lived, and I figured if God could change you, then He could change me too." These harsh words caught me completely off guard and I felt a sudden mix of extreme emotions. I was both angry and ashamed all at once—angry that a close friend would pass such a harsh judgment on me, and ashamed that I had both failed God and let David down in the process.

I learned a tough lesson through that experience: We never know how we might affect others with the choices we make, and this life is not only about us but about those whom we may help or harm by our lifestyles.

The Bible warns us in Romans:

> ... *but rather resolve this, not to put a stum-*
> *bling block or a cause to fall in our brother's*
> *way.* Romans 14:13

That's exactly what I had done to David. I had put a *stumblingblock* and *cause to fall* in my brother's way by the wrong choices I had made.

Worse Than the First

It would have been bad enough if I was now just practicing the same sins I had done before I got saved, but it didn't stop there. When I had gone through deliverance at Brother Glenn's house many months earlier, the Lord had set me free from several evil habits. But when I turned back to my old ways of living, I not only opened myself up again to those ungodly practices, but also to new ones as well.

The Bible explains the process of what happened to me in this way:

> *When an unclean spirit goes out of a man, he goes through dry places, seeking rest; and finding none, he says, "I will return to my house from which I came." ... THEN HE GOES AND TAKES WITH HIM SEVEN OTHER SPIRITS MORE WICKED THAN HIMSELF, and they enter and dwell there; AND THE LAST STATE OF THAT MAN IS WORSE THAN THE FIRST.*
> Luke 11:24-26, Emphasis added

INTO THE SHADOWS

It wasn't long before I began to do things I had sworn never to do. I started to experiment with much stronger drugs, take careless chances I wouldn't have taken before and found myself hanging out with a very dangerous crowd.

Even in my backslidden condition, I would often sense an evil presence when I walked into some places and realize I had to get out of there as quickly as I could. Time proved these impressions correct, when anything from violent acts to drug busts later occurred in some of those very places. Through it all, God had mercy on me, and I was spared any physical harm or jail time.

I was regularly attending rock concerts and parties and kept myself occupied doing everything but the will of God. I dated several girls, but I had no intention of ever settling down. I had no focus and no goal, living only for the moment and whatever pleasure might be found in it.

Then, one day a close friend approached me about sharing the expenses of an apartment. At the time we were both living with our grandmothers, which cramped our lifestyles considerably, so having our own place sounded like a wonderful idea. After all, neither of our grandmothers approved of the things we were doing, so we figured that if we could get out on our own, we could then do whatever we wanted, whenever we wanted to do it. I agreed to the arrangement, and we soon found an affordable place where we could carry on our sinful living.

A Total Loss

Everything seemed to go well for a while, and we were having all the "fun" we wanted, but then our finances began to run low and, before we knew it, we were a month behind on the rent and utilities.

I had long since quit working at the meat market and neither of us was now holding down a regular job, so we depended on occasionally selling drugs to make ends meet. But then the drug supply began to dry up and, to make things worse, we were sharing a lot of the pot we had with friends, so we were actually smoking up our profits. It didn't take long for our loose living to catch up with us, and it all came crashing down at the most inconvenient time.

We had celebrated the Christmas season and New Year in grand fashion, floating from one party to the next, but now it was mid-January, and we were deeper in the hole than ever. The rent was now over two months behind, the landlord was breathing down our necks, and the utilities were about to be turned off for non-payment.

Then, to make matters worse, one day my buddy informed me that, since we couldn't pay the bills, he was moving back to his grandmother's. I really didn't want to give up the apartment, so I held out as long as I could, but things quickly went from bad to worse.

The people I had considered my close friends now had nothing to do with me (since I had no marijuana to offer them), and the girl I had been dating quit coming around. Then, one cold winter night, my life finally reached a turning point.

There was no food left in the apartment, and I had no money left to buy more. My buddy had our only transportation, so when he left, there went my ride. On top of everything else, I had gotten sick and developed a severe case of laryngitis. My throat was almost swollen shut, and I could barely talk or breathe. When I called the doctor, he informed me there was nothing he could do for me.

Coming Home

Everything was falling apart around me, but just when I was ready to throw my hands up in surrender, I got a revelation. It's amazing how sin can blind you to the obvious. At that moment, when I had nothing else left, I realized that I needed to turn back to God.

I looked at the current condition of my life, thinking about how far I had fallen and how much I had left behind when I quit living for God, and I said this simple but sincere prayer: "God, I'm coming home." I was fully aware of what I was saying and meant every word of it. From that moment, I determined to get things right with God, and I began my climb out of the pit.

I believe it's extremely important to point out here that when I first gave my heart to God in 1979, many things instantly fell away in my life. It was amazingly easy. I was truly reborn and could feel I had a new lease on life. But when I came back to God after falling away, everything did not change overnight. Yes, God is merciful and forgiving, but He is also wise.

The long, slow process it took to get me back where I needed to be with God was the best thing He could have done for me. It gave me plenty of time to appreciate how good I'd had it before and to think about what caused me to fall in the first place. It had been a miserable experience and one I did not want to ever repeat.

I had to have a place to live, so the first thing I did was to move in with my grandmother again. I also had to get some employment because I wanted to do what was right, and that meant not only earning money for my daily living, but paying off the debts that had accumulated while I was living irresponsibly. God is always ready to help us out when we honestly want to please Him, and He provided me with a job in remarkable time.

Early one morning I was sitting in a friend's kitchen having breakfast, when my buddy, with whom I had shared the apartment, pulled up in front of the house in a company pickup. He walked up to the door and informed me that the tree service he was working for had just lost an employee and needed someone right away. He didn't know if I wanted a job, but if I did he said I could start to work right then. I didn't even hesitate. "I'll be right with you," I said. "Just let me get my shoes on." It wasn't the easiest job, but I was grateful to get it, and I promptly began to pay off my debts. I knew that God was smiling on me with favor, and suddenly things began looking up.

While I had completely quit drugs and alcohol, I still struggled with some old attitudes and sought God daily to help me be free of them, so that I could serve Him completely. I began to watch the strong-holds fall away and, while I still had a long way to go, I knew I was finally on the road to recovery with God.

Over the next few months I made major headway, and it wasn't long before I began to feel like my relationship with God was returning to where it had been before. I had learned to ignore one of Satan's greatest deceptions—that you have sinned too much for God to ever forgive you. Satan will always try to keep you away from God any way he can, and putting doubt in your mind about God's mercy and grace is one of the most effective weapons he has. You can be assured that Satan will never speak the truth to you regarding God.

Jesus exposed the deceitful nature of Satan in the Gospel of John when He said:

> *There is no truth in him. When he speaks a lie, he speaks from his own resources, for he is a liar and the father of it.*　　　　　John 8:44

> *For there is no truth in him. When he lies, he speaks his native language, for he is a liar and the father of lies.*　　　　　NIV

Chapter 7

BACK IN THE GLORY

But the father said to his servants, "Bring out the best robe and put it on him, and put a ring on his hand and sandals on his feet."

Luke 15:22

This verse is taken from the story of the Prodigal Son, when the father received his wayward child back home, after the son had lost everything while living a life of sin. The ring represented the authority and power that was restored to the prodigal son when he was accepted back into the family as a rightful heir to all his father possessed, and the sandals represented his new, cleansed walk or changed lifestyle.

Like the prodigal son in this story, I lost all I had, but my heavenly Father had lovingly restored my relationship with Him, and now it was time to step back into the authority I had exercised previously as a child of God. It was time to pick up where I had left off in my supernatural journey.

Spiritual Gifts

I was seriously determined to improve my walk with God, so I began to dig deeper into His Word than ever before. Knowing from scripture that our real battle is not with natural enemies that are physically seen but those evil spiritual forces that are unseen (see Ephesians 6:12), I strove to learn more about the spirit realm.

I began to study teachings by several different ministers on what is often referred to as "the Gifts of the Spirit," as recorded in 1 Corinthians 12:

> *There are diversities of gifts, but the same Spirit.*
> *There are differences of ministries, but the same*
> *Lord. And there are diversities of activities, but*
> *it is the same God who works all in all.*
>
> 1 Corinthians 12:4-6

This chapter goes on to list the nine different spiritual gifts that are made available to every believer, when and as God determines, and many theologians group them into three categories: (1) Revelation

Gifts, (2) Power Gifts, and (3) Vocal Gifts. I had operated to a limited degree in some of these gifts already, but I knew there was so much more about them I still didn't understand. One day I became so hungry to know more about the various functions and characteristics of the spiritual gifts that I decided to go on a fast and pray to God for insight.

When we fast, we tune out our natural urges (messages being sent from our body and mind), so that we can more easily tune in to our spiritual urges (messages being sent from our spirit). I started fasting early one morning about 8 a.m. While I was totally abstaining from every type of solid food, I felt in my spirit that it was all right to drink water and an occasional cup of coffee, so around nine that morning I decided to pay a visit to my favorite little cafe.

Many of my Christian friends would often stop in there during lunch, and we had some great times of fun and fellowship while sitting around the tables. Since I got there a little early on this particular day, there was only one customer in the cafe, a young lady. I didn't recognize her, so I walked over and took a seat alone at one of my favorite spots a couple of tables away. The chair I was sitting in was facing her, so I could see the top half of her body above the table unobstructed.

A Glimpse into the Spirit World

I was sitting there sipping on a hot cup of coffee when I happened to glance up at the woman. From across the room I could clearly see several small, bright white lights as they began to appear all over her chest area. The diameter of the lights ranged from about the size of a dime to about the size of a nickel. I watched them for a few seconds, and then they slowly disappeared. Confident that this supernatural experience was a direct response to my prayer and fasting, I got up and walked over to the lady's table in hopes of learning more about what had just happened.

I started off, "I was kind of staring at your blouse a while ago, and I didn't want you to get the wrong idea. I don't know how you believe, but sometimes God will reveal things about someone to another person. When I looked over at you a few moments ago, I saw bright white lights all over your chest. I was just wondering if there is anything wrong with your chest or lungs"

The lady acted naturally surprised at such a statement from a total stranger, but she quickly answered my question: "As a matter of fact, I *do* have problems with my chest. I have severe asthma, and so I have a lot of trouble breathing."

I believed, at this point, that God had already begun to grant my desire to learn more about the gifts of the Spirit. I also believed that He had imparted to me one of the revelation gifts, the word of knowledge, in the form of an open vision with the intent of showing this suffering lady His great power, love and mercy.

I said, "Well, I believe God showed me this because He wants to heal you." Then I asked, "Is it all right if I say a prayer for you right now?"

"Sure," she said.

I began to call on God on the woman's behalf and, as I prayed, I felt the tangible presence of His wonderful Spirit in the form of steady waves of electricity flowing all over my body. When I finished, I asked her how she felt, and she said she could breathe better. I smiled and went back to my own table.

The lady eventually got up and walked out of the room, and I never saw her again. Even though I never found out who she was, I was excited that God had answered my prayer about spiritual gifts so quickly and that He was now using me again in supernatural ways.

Many people believe that they must fast for long periods of time before God will hear or answer them. While I am not discouraging or condemning long fasts, it is important to mention here that I had only been fasting about an hour and a half when this remarkable event occurred. An incident from the book of Daniel appears to support the idea that it is not the length of the fast that causes God to take notice, but rather the condition of the heart.

In this particular account, Daniel had been fasting for twenty-one days when an angel of the Lord appeared to him and gave him this message:

> ... *from the FIRST DAY that you set your heart to understand, and to humble yourself before your God, your words were heard.*
> Daniel 10:12, Emphasis added

It was Daniel's humble heart that was the key to an audience with God. The chapter goes on to say that the reason it took so long for the angel to get the message to Daniel was because a ruling evil spirit, called *"the prince of the kingdom of Persia"* (Daniel 10:13), had detained the angel for twenty-one days. It is God's desire to respond to our prayers, but Satan will do all that he can to prevent our answer from arriving.

During a time of waiting for an answer, the old deceiver will begin to sow seeds of doubt in our minds. He will try to get us to doubt God's ability to answer our prayers and meet our needs. Worst of all, Satan will try to get us to doubt God's love for us. If we begin to doubt that God cares, the devil knows that he has a chance to get us and keep us away from the things of God.

No Better than Demons

One day I was taking a casual drive around my hometown when I decided to swing by the local Sonic and grab a cold Dr. Pepper. I pulled into one of the stalls to order my drink, and as soon as I stopped the car, the Lord spoke something into my heart: "Dale is getting ready to pull in beside you, and when he does, I want you to go talk to him."

I had known Dale for many years, and we had always been close friends. I had witnessed to him on several occasions about God's marvelous power, love and forgiveness, and while he always seemed to show some interest, my messages never seemed to hit home with him. This day would be different.

The Lord went on to give me a play-by-play rundown of how our conversation would go: "Go over to Dale and ask him if he thinks he's going to Heaven," He said. Then He continued, "He will say, 'Yes.' Then ask him why he believes that. He will say, 'Because I believe in God.' "

The Lord continued, "Open your Bible and have him read James 2:19, and then ask him what he thinks that scripture means." Revelation knowledge is one of the most amazing gifts that God makes available to His children. It gives us supernatural insight and sometimes, as in this incident, foreknowledge to help us know how to conduct an effective conversation. But, it can also help us touch the soul. In this case, it was going to help open the eyes of a person God loved and wanted to reach.

Just as God had said, Dale came driving around the corner just seconds later and pulled into the Sonic driveway. He could have picked any of several open stalls, but, instead, he pulled into the one right next to me.

Once Dale was parked, I took my Bible and walked over to his car. I knew him well enough to invite myself into his car, so I opened the front passenger's side door, got in and took a seat.

I wasted no time in asking Dale the questions the Lord had told me to ask, and, sure enough, he replied exactly as the Lord had said he would.

As instructed, I then asked Dale to read the following scripture from the book of James:

> *You believe that there is one God. You do well. Even the demons believe—and tremble!*
>
> James 2:19

When Dale had finished reading, I did as I was told and asked him what he thought that scripture meant. "It means I'm no better than a demon!" he replied. The look of surprise on Dale's face made it clear that he had received a shocking revelation. He now realized that going to Heaven would require much more of him than mere belief in God's existence.

Actually, Dale was really no different than countless other people all over the world. Throughout the ages, men and women have reduced their understanding of God down to an intellectual level. But God is a Spirit, and the only way to gain access to Him and to Heaven is to approach Him on a spiritual level. It is only as we first come into a personal relationship with God's Son, Jesus, that we can have open access to the Father.

Jesus said very emphatically:

I am the way, the truth, and the life. No one comes to the Father except through Me.   John 14:6

He Knows Your Thoughts

I remember attending church one Sunday evening with a couple of friends of mine, and after the service we decided to go to a local Braum's Ice Cream & Dairy Store and have a dessert. On the way, I was sitting in the back seat, and as we traveled along, I leaned forward and began to share with my friends some of the wonderful supernatural ways in which God had been using me lately.

Fay was sitting on the passenger's side in the front, and her boyfriend was driving. I could see Fay plainly, and no sooner had I finished speaking than I clearly heard her say, "I wish God would use me that way."

Although I never saw her lips move, I distinctly heard those words, as if she had spoken them out loud. I was so convinced of what I had just heard that I turned to Fay and said, "God *will* use you. All you have to do is believe."

She turned her head toward me and, with an astonished look on her face, asked, "Why did you say that?"

I said, "Isn't that what you were thinking?"

"Yes," she admitted, "but I never said anything. How did you know that's what I was thinking?"

"Because I *heard* your thoughts," I replied.

We have an example of this type of supernatural occurrence in the book of Matthew, where it is recorded that Jesus *knew* men's thoughts:

> *And at once some of the Pharisees SAID WITHIN THEMSELVES, "This Man blasphemes!"*
> *But Jesus, KNOWING THEIR THOUGHTS, said, "Why do you THINK evil IN YOUR HEARTS?"*
> Matthew 9:3-4, Emphasis added

The phrase used here, "*said within themselves,*" means that the Pharisees were thinking this, but didn't say it out loud.

Another case of Jesus knowing men's thoughts is recorded in Luke 11:16-17.

> *Others, testing Him, sought from Him a sign from heaven. But He, KNOWING THEIR THOUGHTS, said to them ... .*
> Luke 11:16-17, Emphasis added

The word *testing* used in this verse means that the people were trying to manipulate Jesus into doing something. They were using deception to trick Him, but Jesus knew their real intent because He could read their thoughts.

Jesus said that He was one with God the Father, and Psalm 94 states:

> *The LORD knows the thoughts of man.*
>   Psalm 94:11

In a request to God concerning His disciples, Jesus said this prayer, as we noted earlier:

> *... that they all may be one; as you, Father, are in Me, and I in You; that they also they may be one in Us, that the world may believe that You sent Me.*   John 17:21

If the Lord knows the thoughts of men, and we are one with Him, then we, too, can know the thoughts of men when God desires it.

Jesus also said, as noted, to His disciples:

> *Most assuredly, I say to you, he who believes in Me, the works that I do he will do also.*   John 14:12

Jesus was able to know men's thoughts through the power of the Holy Spirit indwelling Him, and, according to this scripture, Christians are capable of experiencing some of the same supernatural manifestations of God that Jesus did.

One of the nine spiritual gifts mentioned in 1 Corinthians 12, which is available to all believers as the Holy Spirit wills, is the word of knowledge. This is the ability to supernaturally know facts about people, places and things, just as Jesus did.

In my particular case, the Lord was temporarily granting me the ability, through the word of knowledge, to hear the longing of this woman's heart.

I have found that God always has practical reasons for the things He does, and I believe He had a two-fold purpose in this particular supernatural manifestation of His Great Spirit:

1. It was meant to build up my own level of faith and understanding in the gifts of the Spirit.

2. More importantly, it occurred to give Fay assurance that God knew her personally and loved her enough to take the time to respond concerning the cry of her heart.

Go to the Well

When I share with others the story of how I back-slid and went away from the Lord, people often ask me if I know what caused it. I always tell them it was two main things:

1. Thinking that I would not be affected by constantly hanging out with sinners.

2. Failing to maintain fellowship with and draw strength from other Christians.

With those two bitter lessons on my mind, I quickly set about to find a church where I could fellowship with like-minded believers. I was thrilled to discover that a new church had just started up right there in my hometown. Faith Christian Cathedral became a true spiritual oasis for me, and I met a lot of new people there, people who quickly became very close friends.

During one particular service, Pastor Ken announced an upcoming fellowship dinner, to be held at the home of one of the church members. When the scheduled day finally arrived, we all showed up at that person's house and had a great evening of good food and warm fellowship.

While we were all visiting in the game room that night, I noticed an unfamiliar lady standing near the couch. I assumed that she had been invited by someone in the church, since I had never seen her before. As I glanced over at her, these words seemed to rise up from deep inside of me, "Go to the well."

I didn't know what this might mean, so I brushed it aside. I struck up a conversation with someone standing nearby, but it wasn't long before the same words came to me again, "Go to the well."

This time I felt an urge to tell the words to the unfamiliar woman I had seen moments before. I felt a little awkward telling this to a perfect stranger, especially since I had no idea what it meant or if she would even receive it, so I brushed the thought aside again.

When the same words came back to me a third time, accompanied by an even stronger urge to tell her, I finally gave in and approached her rather cautiously. "Excuse me," I began. "I don't know you, but as I was looking at you a few minutes ago, I felt like God gave me some words He wanted me to share with you."

What happened next caught me by complete surprise. Not only did I deliver the words I had originally heard, but as I spoke, God interjected even more words into the message. I said to her, "Go to the well. The well has water. The water is the Word."

I had no more expected this to happen than to be the first man on the moon, but I have since learned that is exactly how God will lead us many times when delivering a message. He gives us something to begin with, and then, as we obey His leading, He provides more along the way.

We find a perfect example of this in 2 Kings 9:1-10 where *"one of the sons of the prophets"* (verse 1) was instructed by Elisha to deliver a few words to King Jehu. While the young man was speaking, the Lord added considerably more to the content of the original message.

This is really a matter of faith. You step out with what you have, and God will be there to meet you. This is much like what happened to Peter when Jesus told him to step out onto the sea, and when he did, Jesus was there to keep him from sinking.

After I said those words, I told the lady, "I don't know if that means anything to you, but I believe God wanted me to share it with you."

She didn't confirm it one way or the other, so I excused myself, walked back over to the person I had been talking to previously, and resumed our conversation. A few minutes later Pastor Ken asked if there was anyone who had anything they would like to share. The lady whom I had given the message to spoke up and said she had something she wanted to say.

I must admit I was a little apprehensive, thinking I might have offended the woman in some way. But what she said next brought me both joy and relief.

"I don't know who this young man is," she said, pointing over at me, "but he just said some words to me that was an answer to my prayer.

"You see, I got saved not too long ago, and I have been reading the Bible a lot. But my mother has been telling me that reading the Bible too much could make me go crazy, so I would have to quit reading.

"I had prayed to God to let me know if I was reading too much, and this young man just told me God wanted me to go to His Word. I'm going to start reading again like I was before."

It's a shame to say, but Satan will often use those closest to us to keep us from the good things of God, and we must closely guard our relationship with Him and not listen to any advice that is contrary to His Word or will for our lives. God is so good and, as in this lady's case, He will help and guide us when we are young and inexperienced in spiritual matters. He is always ready to give a kind and encouraging word, and if you are sensitive to His leading, He will even use you to deliver the message. What an honor and privilege to be chosen to serve as God's voice and make a positive impact on someone's life.

Lord, I Need a Sign

A few weeks later I had some business to take care of in downtown Oklahoma City, and I asked my friend, Merrell, if he would like to go along with me. Once we arrived in Oklahoma City, we took an exit off Interstate 40 and headed north up Robinson Avenue. We had only traveled a few blocks when we noticed a man standing on the sidewalk next to the road carrying a large sandwich sign.

As we got closer, we could clearly read a quote from the Bible on one side of the obviously hand-painted sign. We were so impressed with this man's boldness and devotion to spread the Word of God that we just had to go back and tell him. We swung the car around, and once we had parked, we walked over to him and struck up a conversation. He told us he had been doing this for years, and it was just his way of spreading the Gospel.

I asked the man if there was anything we could do for him. He said the thick plywood signs he carried were very heavy and he had to use several of them in order to share multiple scriptures. He said he really wished he could get a lighter sign that was made in such a way that he could change the letters out instead of having to hand-paint a different message on several different signs. I told him I didn't have money to buy him a sign, but I would be willing to pray for Him. (People who think they are unable to help others often underestimate the power that is available to them through prayer.)

In Acts 3, a story is recorded about Peter and John who met a lame beggar while on their way to the temple. The man asked the apostles for a handout, but Peter didn't have any money. The average person might have given up at that point, but not Peter. He knew he was not limited by his own resources because he had faith in a God who was more than enough. This was Peter's response to the beggar:

> *"Silver and gold I do not have, but what I do have I give you: In the name of Jesus Christ of Nazareth, rise up and walk." And he took him by the right hand and lifted him up, and immediately his feet and ankle bones received*

strength. So he, leaping up, stood and walked
and entered the temple with them—walking
and leaping and praising God. Acts 3:6-8

I had seen the Lord provide some remarkable answers to prayer up to that time, and my faith was at high tide. I told this gentleman that he was doing a very good thing by sharing the Word on a busy street, and I was confident the Lord wanted to help him. He joined hands with Merrell and me, and we prayed right there in downtown Oklahoma City, as the afternoon traffic sped by.

"Lord," I began. "You said in Matthew 18:19 (KJV), *'If two of you shall agree on earth as touching anything that they shall ask, it shall be done for them of my Father which is in Heaven.'* Now, Lord, You see that this man is trying to spread the Gospel, and he needs a better sign. So, I stand in agreement with him that You are going to make a way for him to have what he needs, and I thank You for it in Jesus' name. Amen!"

I then turned to the man and said, "Brother, I believe God heard us, and He's going to give you what you need."

We stood there visiting for what couldn't have been more than a minute when a pickup passed by that had some type of lettering on the door. It traveled about a block and then turned around. As it approached, it pulled over next to the curb beside us, and the driver rolled down his window. He explained to the man with the signs that he greatly respected what he was doing and would like to help him out. He said (you guessed it), "I own a company that makes plastic signs, and I would like to provide one for you. You can change out the lettering on it when you add a new message, and that way you won't have to carry all those heavy wooden signs around."

"But I don't have the money to pay for one like that," the gentleman told the driver.

"You don't have to," the driver explained. "They're free, and I'll give you as many as you want for as long as you need them."

There really is power in agreement, and God is true to His Word. If we will do our part, He is faithful to do His.

The Bible reassures us:

And whatever we ask we receive of Him, because we keep His commandments and do those things that are pleasing in His sight.
1 John 3:22

A Warrior Angel

The night I first met those evangelists at Brother Glenn's house, I had no idea they would become such valued friends. I believed they were chosen by God to introduce me to the deeper things of His Spirit, but I really doubted whether I would ever see them again.

After I returned to my home in Oklahoma, I was informed that they sometimes spoke at different venues around the state, so I made every effort to attend their meetings as often as I could. Over time we became very well acquainted, and I even had the distinct honor of visiting their home in Wichita Falls, Texas on various occasions. During one such visit, I had a supernatural encounter that would broaden my understanding of the Spirit world tremendously.

That day had been especially busy at their house, and it was now late in the evening. Most of the family had gone to bed, but Sister A. and her oldest daughter were seated in chairs at one end of the living room next to the kitchen door, and I was at the other end of the living room, relaxing in a large arm chair, facing the two of them. Since it was so late, most of the lights in the house were out except the ceiling light in the kitchen.

While I sat there casually listening to the conversation at the other end of the room, I suddenly caught some movement out of the corner of my right eye. I slowly turned to see what it was. There, just inside the front door, I saw what appeared to be a group of small white lights that looked very much like sparkling glitter. Since it was heavily shadowed in that part of the house, the sparkling lights stood out very distinctly against the dark background.

I thought surely that Sister A. and her daughter were seeing the same thing, since they were actually in a more direct line of sight to the front door than I was. Yet, when I looked over to where they were seated, it became obvious that they were completely unaware of what was going on before my eyes.

I looked back over toward the front door once again and realized that the lights were growing in number and had even begun to take on the shape of a man—a very large man.

The average door in a home is about seven feet tall and three feet wide. The shape I was seeing reached from the floor to just above the door frame and filled the entryway from side to side. While I wasn't able to distinguish any fine details, there was no mistaking the outline of a head, very broad shoulders, large arms that hung to the side, and the full length of a masculine body.

This vision was to my right, and the whole time I was looking at it, the entire right side of my body was charged with electricity, and the hair on my right arm stood straight up. Just like the time I had seen the bright light in front of the cross at the Methodist Church back in Pauls Valley, I felt absolutely no fear at this supernatural appearance. As I continued to watch it, the sparkling figure slowly began to fade, and the lights soon vanished completely.

I wasn't sure what had just happened, exactly why it took place, nor why Sister A. and her daughter weren't able to see the bright, supernatural vision that manifested directly in front of them.

Before we went to bed, I told Sister A. what I had witnessed, but she didn't seem to have much to say about it at the time. Then, the next morning, she told me something that brought me a much greater understanding of what had occurred the night before.

"What you didn't know, Jim," she began, "was that we've had a prowler around the neighborhood for the last several nights before you came. I know I should have had more faith in God," she humbly confessed, "but I have to admit, I have been scared.

"I have not been able to sleep well, and it was starting to affect my health. I was praying to God to do something, and the night you told me you saw that vision I knew it was an angel that the Lord had sent to protect us," she explained.

"Last night I slept better than I had in several nights, and it was because of the vision you told me you saw."

Now I knew what I had seen and why I had seen it, but I still didn't know why I was the only who was able to see it. Sister A's response was, " I don't know why no one else saw the angel, Jim. I guess that's just the way God wanted it."

The Bible is full of stories where angels of God intervened in the affairs of mankind and many times offered them help in time of need. We are told in Hebrews:

> *Are they* [angels] *not all ministering spirits sent forth to minister for those who will inherit salvation?* Hebrews 1:14

Again, the Bible promises in Psalms:

> *The angel of the LORD encamps all around those who fear Him,*
> *And delivers them.* Psalm 34:7

While I now certainly believed in the existence of angels, I still wanted to receive some sort of confirmation from God concerning my particular experience. After all, I had heard of angels with robes and angels with wings, but never angels that appeared as sparkling light.

When sharing this experience with others, I have often been asked to describe more precisely how the image of light first appeared. I have always responded with the best example I could think of from a personal viewpoint. "Have you ever seen Star Trek," I ask, "where Captain Kirk would stand in the transporter room and say, 'Beam me up, Scotty'? The molecules in his body would begin to break down, and it looked like shimmering, sparkling light. Well, that's the way the image came, and that's the way it left."

I continued to pray that God would verify that what I had seen was, in fact, one of His heavenly beings, but it wasn't until several years later that I received a confirmation with which I was satisfied.

I was working as a desk clerk at a local hotel back in my hometown in Oklahoma one Saturday when the manager, Carol, dropped in to check on things. I noticed the shopping bag in her hand and asked her where she had been. She explained that she had just returned from Mardel's Christian Book Store, where she had picked up a few books, so I asked to see what she had bought. One of the books, *The Man Who Talked with Angels,* [6] was written by a woman named Sharon Rose Buck White. Her father, Pastor Roland Buck, had written a book some years earlier entitled *Angels on Assignment,* [7] in which he described, in remarkable detail, numerous angelic visitations he claimed to have encountered over a period of several months.

Since the publication of the first book, Pastor Buck had passed away, and this more-recent volume, put together by his daughter, was actually a sequel to her father's best-seller. In her book, Mrs. White shares with the readers accounts of the last nine angelic visitations her father had, accounts not included in the pages of *Angels on Assignment.*

In Mrs. White's book, I found the confirmation I had been looking for concerning my amazing encounter in Wichita Falls. In chapter 25, she gives her father's account of the very last angelic encounter he had, less than a month before he went to Heaven. To my delight and relief, there, on the pages before me, was Pastor Buck's unique description of what transpired on the evening of October 13, 1979.

6. Documentation unknown
7. Houston, Texas (Hunter Books: 1979)

"Last night, in my office, I found out that the visit six weeks ago wasn't the last one ... . My head was down, and I was doing some meditating, and looking at the Scriptures," Pastor Buck recalled. "They came in just like those people on the television series, 'Star Trek.' I was breathless because I never get accustomed to their presence."

"Star Trek" ... there it was. Those key words jumped out at me and settled the issue forever in my mind. It was a unique description of a very unique experience, unlike anything else I had ever known up to that time. Although I don't know why God took so long to confirm my experience, I no longer doubted that I had seen an actual angel late that night in the ministers' home.

Many people live an entire lifetime and never see an angel, so I was very grateful for this rare opportunity God had allowed. But this was not to be the only time I would be permitted to catch a glimpse of God's heavenly hosts.

God's View of Catholics

Several months passed by, and one weekend I decided to pay Sister A. and her family another visit in Wichita Falls. While I was there, one afternoon their oldest daughter was getting ready to go to the grocery store to pick up a few things for dinner, and she asked me if I would like to go along with her and see the neighborhood. I accepted.

Our trip to the store was normal enough, but on the way back to their house something totally unexpected and very unusual happened. As we left a housing area and entered a clearing, I noticed some one-story office buildings about a block away to my right. I was wondering what the structures might be when suddenly, about a hundred feet directly above the buildings, the clear blue sky became instantly filled with a vast number of bright flashes of pure white light.

This sight reminded me of the multiple camera flashes that go off when swarms of paparazzi are covering a major celebrity event in Hollywood. Curious to what this might mean, I turned to the young lady beside me and asked her what those buildings were. "That's a Catholic school," she replied. (I later learned that it was Notre Dame Catholic School). Suddenly, I felt strong waves of power begin to sweep over me like electricity, and my senses were heightened until I felt more alert than I had ever been in my life.

About that time I heard God speak some words

inside of me that would result in a major adjust-ment to my theology. "This is what it will feel like when you are operating in the gift of discerning of spirits. [8] The flashes you are seeing over the school are the guardian angels assigned to the children that attend there," the Spirit of God said.

That explanation gave me understanding into what I had just encountered in the Spirit realm, but the following words gave me insight into the very heart of God. "I love the Catholics," I clearly heard the Lord say next. This statement was especially important to me because I had heard a lot of negative comments about Catholics over the years, and I really wondered how God felt about them.

It wasn't just God's choice of words that moved me that day; it was also the warmth that I sensed coming from His heart to mine toward Catholics. As He spoke, I heard a gentle absoluteness in His voice that I knew was intended to settle the issue in my mind once and for all. While I firmly be-lieve that some denominations do have a greater grasp of spiritual truth than others, I am also totally convinced that God loves all people, and it is His desire that believers all over the world

8. See 1 Corinthians 12:10

should come into the unity of the faith of Jesus Christ.

There is power in numbers, and the enemy of our souls knows that division is one of the most effective weapons he can use against the Body of Christ. In the New Testament, the Bible clearly points out the adverse effects of division:

> *If a kingdom is divided AGAINST ITSELF, that kingdom cannot stand. And if a house is divided AGAINST ITSELF, that house cannot stand.* Mark 3:24-25, Emphasis added

The devil knows full well what division can do. First, division brings ridicule on the Body of Christ from those on the outside who observe our foolish bickering and quarreling. Those who might otherwise consider becoming a Christian often change their minds when they see our outrageous behavior toward one another. After all, who wants to be involved with people who claim to serve the God of love and yet cannot seem to get along? That's why we are often (rightly) accused of being hypocrites—people who profess to believe in one thing yet practice the exact opposite.

Second, division makes it hard, if not impossible, to launch unified efforts to spread the Gospel and meet the material needs of lost and dying people all around the world.

Passages from the Old Testament show us how very special unity is to God:

> *Behold, how good and how pleasant it is*
> *For brethren to dwell together in unity!*
> *It is like the precious oil upon the head,*
> *Running down on the beard,*
> *The beard of Aaron,*
> *Running down on the edge of his garments.*
> *It is like the dew of Hermon,*
> *Descending upon the mountains of Zion;*
> *For there the Lord commanded the blessing —*
> *Life for evermore.*   Psalm 133:1-3

Here God described unity as *"good," "pleasant"* and *"precious."* As a result of this unity, it says He *"commanded the blessing"* which was *"life for evermore."* These scriptures should serve as a great motivation for all of us to seek unity in the faith of Jesus Christ with all our heart.

The Story Continues

I have now shared with you several supernatural encounters in this book, but the Lord has allowed me to experience many more amazing things over the years—far too many to cover in one volume. In future books, I will share many more stories, as well as specifics on topics that will help you live the abundant life that Jesus has made available. I will also reveal many more of the wonderful truths the Lord has taught me over the last four decades, truths such as:

1. How we can recognize demonic activity and what to do about it.
2. How we can know God's peace, love and joy in a far greater measure—even in the midst of trials and trouble.
3. How to recognize God's leading so we don't miss the blessings He's trying to provide for us and our loved ones.

4. The incredible countless ways God answers prayer that will build your faith and trust in Jehovah Jireh, God the Provider.
5. How to effectively pray for your loved ones when they don't seem interested in the things of God.
6. How you can know and walk in the supernatural power of God.
7. How to receive God's blessing in the classroom and the workplace.

Acknowledgements

Thanks to my Sunday School teacher, Gene Williams, who taught me the books of the Bible and planted the seed of salvation in my soul at an early age.

Thanks to Brother Glenn, who introduced me to the ministry of deliverance and helped me to realize what it meant to be "free indeed."

Thanks to Rev. Jimmy Dehart, who befriended me when I was still a diamond in the rough and has remained a steadfast friend over the years.

Thanks to my beloved former pastors, Charles and Wanda McKay, who recognized the calling on my life and allowed me the opportunity to exercise the spiritual gifts God has given me.

Thanks to the following ministers, Kenneth E. Hagin, Pat Robertson, Lester Sumrall, Norvel Hayes,

Kenneth Copeland, Gary Greenwald, Bill Hamon, Rita Phillips, Chuck Pierce, Sid Roth, Paul Crouch and the many others God has used in a very special way over the years to help me better understand and operate more effectively in the Spirit realm.

Thanks to my wife, family members and friends who offered their continued support and encouragement, which helped me to see this project through to the end.

Special thanks to Harold McDougal for his patience and guidance during the editing process of this book.

Most of all, thanks be to an awesome God who gave His only Son to be a sacrifice for my sins so that I could experience His great love and power and be called:

Out of Darkness

— Suggested Reading —

Books by Kenneth E. Hagin

1. I Believe in Visions
2. The Believer's Authority
3. The Holy Spirit and His Gifts
4. Tongues: Beyond the Upper Room

Books by Dr. Bill Hamon

1. Prophets and Personal Prophecy: God's Prophetic Voice Today
2. Prophets and the Prophetic Movement: God's Prophetic Move Today
3. Prophets, Pitfalls and Principles: God's Prophetic People Today
4. Seventy Reasons for Speaking in Tongues

Books by Jane Hamon

1. The Deborah Company: Becoming a Woman Who Makes a Difference
2. Dreams & Visions: Understanding and Interpreting God's Messages to You

Books by John G. Lake

1. Adventures in God
2. Your Power in the Holy Spirit

Books by Smith Wigglesworth

1. Healing
2. The Power to Serve
3. Ever Increasing Faith

Author Contact Information

You may contact the author in the following ways:

Jim O. Richardson
PO Box 277
Pauls Valley, OK 73075

e-mail: jimrich1951@yahoo.com

www.ingramcontent.com/pod-product-compliance
Lightning Source LLC
LaVergne TN
LVHW011330080426
835513LV00006B/277